Why It Matters- Finding Hope in Moments of Frustration"

Joshua Rhoades

Published by Joshua Paul Rhoades, 2024.

While every precaution has been taken in the preparation of this book, the publisher assumes no responsibility for errors or omissions, or for damages resulting from the use of the information contained herein.

WHY IT MATTERS- FINDING HOPE IN MOMENTS OF FRUSTRATION"

First edition. November 25, 2024.

Copyright © 2024 Joshua Rhoades.

ISBN: 979-8227681188

Written by Joshua Rhoades.

Also by Joshua Rhoades

Courage Under Fire: David's Stand On The Battlefield
Jonah's Journey: Voices Of Redemption And Lessons In Obedience
The Furnace Of Faith: 12 Principles From The Heat Of Faith
Whispers of Hope: Inspiring Stories of Men's Prayers In Scripture
Frontier Legends: The Oregon Dream
Elijah: A Beacon Of Boldness
HOOK, LINE & SAVIOUR - Faith Reflections from Fishing
Driven By Faith: Motor Racing Inspired Christian Life
30 Day Devotional - Bold and Strong- Coffee Devotions for a Courageous Christian Walk
Authentic Christianity: The Heart of Old Time Religion
Consider The Ant - God's Tiny Preachers
Flee Fornication: The Plea For Purity
Renewed Hope- How to Find Encouragement in God
Sounding The Call - The Voice of Conviction
The Altar - Where Heaven Meets Earth
The Bible's Battlefields- Timeless Lessons from Ancient Wars
The Sacred Art of Silence - How Silence Speaks in Scripture
Under Fire- The Sanctity of the Traditional Biblical Home
Who Is on the Lord's Side? A Call to Righteousness
What Is Truth? - From Skepticism to Submission
First and Goal- Faith and Football Fundamentals
From Dugout to Devotion- Spiritual Lessons from Baseball
Par for the Course- Faith and Fairways
The Believer's Pace- Tools for Running Life's Marathon
The Immutable Fortress- Security in God's Unchanging Nature
Biblical Bravery
Deer Stands and Devotions: A Hunter's Walk with God

Jesus Knows- Our Hearts, Our Responsibility
Restoration - Setting The Bone
Spiritual 911- God's Word for Life's Emergency's
The Freedom of Forgiveness
The Jezebel Effect - Ancient Manipulations Modern Lessons
The Shout That Stopped The Saviour
The Time Machine Chronicles: Old Testament Characters
Anchored In Truth Exploring The Depths of Psalm 119
Biblical Counsel on Anger
Proverbs' Portraits The Men God Mentions
Stumbling in the Dark - The Dangers of Alcohol
Guarding the Wicket Protecting Your Faith and Game
The Champion's Faith - Wrestling and Achieving Spiritual Victory
Scriptural Commands for Modern Times Living God's Word Today Volume 1
Scriptural Commands for Modern Times Living God's Word Today Volume 2
Scriptural Commands for Modern Times Living God's Word TodayVolume3
The Greatest Gift
A Christmas Journey of Faith
Daughter Of The King: Embracing Your Identity In Christ
Determination and Dedication Building Strong Faith As A Young Man
Walking Through Walls God's Power to Part the Storms of Life
David's Song Of Deliverance Praising God Through Every Storm
From Weakness to Warrior: Gideon's Transformation
Why Did Jesus Weep?
Living For God The Call To Be A Living Sacrifice
My Mind Is In A Fog What Do I Do?
Turning The Page Written By Grace
The Calling and Greatness of John the Baptist
For Such a Time Esther's Courageous Stand
From Brokenness To Beauty Written By The Pen of Grace
The Ultimate Guide to Massive Action- From Plans to Reality
A Heart Of Conviction
Serving In The Shadows
Repentance Revealed The Road Back To God
The Chief Sinner Meets The Chief Saviour Reflections On I Timothy 1:15

Answer The Call - 31 Days of Biblical Action
The Birthmark of the Believer
Reflections on Calvary's Cross
The Kingdom Builder Paul's Bold Proclamation of Christ
The Animal Of Pride
The Reach That Restores Christ Love For The Broken
Paul- The Many Roles of a Servant of Christ
Unshakeable Faith- 31 Days of Peace in God's Word
O Come, Let Us Adore Him- A Christmas Devotional
The Shepherd's Voice
The Trail From Vision To Mission
Enabled- Living God's Purpose With Power
Held Back But Not Defeated
The Enoch Walk
The Power and Precision of God's Word
The Children Who Found Christmas
Why It Matters- Finding Hope in Moments of Frustration"

Dedication

To you, dear reader,

This book is for you. For the one who has ever felt the weight of frustration pressing heavy on your heart. For the one who has cried silent tears in the darkness, wondering if anyone sees, if anyone cares, if any of this pain has meaning. For the one who has felt stuck, lost, or broken, desperately longing for a way forward but unsure if hope still remains.

This is for the one who has whispered, "Why, God?" while staring at shattered pieces of dreams you once held so close. For the one who has felt abandoned by joy, wrestling with the ache of unmet expectations and the sting of silence. You know what it's like to give your all—your time, your energy, your prayers—only to watch everything unravel. And yet, even in the depth of your struggle, you've held onto a faint, flickering desire to believe there's a greater purpose behind it all.

This book is dedicated to the brave heart that still beats within you, even when it feels weary. To the soul that has endured storms you thought would break you but has somehow kept going. To the spirit that longs for more—more peace, more joy, more hope, even in the midst of life's relentless challenges.

You are not forgotten. Your struggles are not unseen. The pain you've carried is not wasted. And though it may feel like your story is marked only by heartache, there is a greater Author at work, writing something beautiful on the pages of your life.

This journey we're embarking on together is about uncovering the sacredness in the struggle. It's about discovering that your moments of frustration are not just random or meaningless—they are spaces where God is working, shaping, refining, and preparing you for something greater than you can imagine. Through the Word of God and the truths of Scripture, this book will guide you to see His fingerprints on even the most painful parts of your journey.

It's okay to feel tired. It's okay to feel unsure. It's okay to not have all the answers. But as you turn these pages, may you feel an undeniable sense of hope rise within you. Hope that God is not only present in your frustration but is using it for your good. Hope that the tears you've shed are watering seeds of growth you cannot yet see. Hope that what seems like a dead end is, in fact, the beginning of a new and beautiful chapter.

You are stronger than you think. The resilience you've shown to even pick up this book is a testament to the courage that already exists within you. And while the road ahead may not always be easy, you don't have to walk it alone. God is with you, and His love is a constant thread weaving through every moment, every heartache, and every triumph.

This dedication is for the times you've felt overwhelmed and for the moments you've stood in the face of adversity and kept going. It's for the prayers you've whispered through tears and the dreams you've dared to hold onto, even when they felt out of reach.

Let this book remind you that you are seen. You are loved. You are never alone. And no matter how impossible the journey may feel, there is hope waiting for you on the other side of frustration.

To the weary, may you find rest.

To the broken, may you find healing.

To the discouraged, may you find the courage to believe again.

To the frustrated, may you find peace.

This is not the end of your story. It's the beginning of something sacred, something extraordinary. God is not finished with you yet, and His plans for you are good. So take a deep breath, hold on, and let's walk this path together.

With all my heart, this is for you.

Dedicated to the reader who still hopes, still searches, and still believes, even in the smallest of ways. You are not forgotten, and you are deeply loved.

Let's discover together why it matters.

In the depths of frustration lies the whisper of hope—a reminder that every tear, every trial, and every unanswered question is part of a more extraordinary story. Trust the process, hold onto faith in the Lord, and know that even in the struggle, Almighty God is shaping you for something exceptional.

Introduction

Day 1 - Perseverance in the Face of Setbacks
Day 2 - Purpose Beyond the Pain
Day 3 - Patience When Progress is Slow
Day 4 - Pushing Through the Pressure
Day 5 - Peace in the Midst of Uncertainty
Day 6 - Persistence When Hope Feels Thin
Day 7 - Perspective on Purposeful Struggles
Day 8 - Power in Staying the Course
Day 9 - Pathways to Peaceful Resolve
Day 10 - Promise in the Process
Day 11 - Prayers for Endurance and Strength
Day 12 - Perceiving Hidden Progress
Day 13 - Preparation Through Life's Trials
Day 14 - Presence Over Perfection
Day 15 - Possibility in Unexpected Places
Day 16 - Proof of Purpose Through Perseverance
Day 17 - Patterns of Growth in Adversity
Day 18 - Pressing On When the Way is Hard
Day 19 - Purifying Purpose in the Struggle
Day 20 - Precious Lessons from Hard Times
Day 21 - Provision in Moments of Doubt
Day 22 - Patient Endurance Amidst Delays
Day 23 - Pillars of Strength and Resilience
Day 24 - Promises Kept in the Dark Times
Day 25 - Prioritizing Faith Over Frustration
Day 26 - Powerful Lessons from Small Wins
Day 27 - Persistence Beyond Visible Progress

Day 28 - Potential Unlocked Through Patience
Day 29 - Proof That the Journey Matters
Day 30 - Planting Seeds of Hope in Struggle
Day 31 - Pathways to Renewal Through Perseverance
Conclusion

Introduction

Welcome to "Why It Matters: Finding Hope in Moments of Frustration". If you're here, you probably know what it feels like to be caught in life's relentless waves, trying to keep your head above water as frustrations tug at your resolve. You may know the feeling of pouring everything you have into something—a relationship, a dream, a season of waiting—and then watching it unravel. You know what it's like to ask, "Does this even matter?" or to cry out, "Why, God?" while staring down a road that seems endless and unyielding. In these moments, hope can feel distant, like a faint whisper amid a roaring storm, and yet somewhere deep inside, you long to believe there is purpose in the struggle—that this frustration, this season, isn't without meaning.

This book was born from the reality of these moments. It's about uncovering the glimmers of hope when the days feel dark and about learning to see the sacredness within the struggle. This journey is for those who have ever felt discouraged, tired, or ready to give up. Together, we'll look at what it means to keep going when life feels heavy, to reach for hope when you're on the verge of letting go, and to find purpose in the very experiences that have left you questioning it all.

Through Scripture and honest reflection, "Why It Matters" will guide you through the beauty of holding on to hope, even when circumstances feel unbearable. You'll see how others have navigated the long, uncertain stretches of frustration and how their faith carried them through. We'll explore the resilience that God builds within us when we face adversity, and how each trial refines us, deepens our faith, and prepares us for what's to come. You'll discover that our struggles aren't wasted—that they are shaping us, drawing us closer to God, and revealing His grace in ways we may have overlooked.

As we walk through these pages, we'll look deeply at how God uses our frustrations to transform us. We'll see that He doesn't waste our pain; He uses every tear, every prayer, every moment of waiting to write a story of redemption and growth. Each step we take, even when it feels small or insignificant, is part of a greater journey. God is with us, even when we feel we're standing still, and He is weaving together each moment to create something beautiful in His perfect timing.

So, if you're ready to discover the hope that lies within your deepest struggles, if you're willing to lean into the possibility that God is at work even in your frustration, then let's begin. This isn't just a book; it's an invitation to journey through the places where faith is tested and to discover why it all matters. There is hope on the other side of frustration. Let's find it together.

Day 1 - Perseverance in the Face of Setbacks

In life, we all face moments of frustration and discouragement, times when it feels like every effort leads to nothing but setbacks and obstacles, making us wonder why we should even keep trying. But when we look to the Bible, we find a message of hope and encouragement that reminds us why perseverance in the face of setbacks truly matters. The Bible tells us over and over that trials and challenges have a purpose in our lives, that they aren't just random difficulties, but moments where God is working something good in us, even if we can't see it right away. In James 1:3-4, we are reminded, "Knowing this, that the trying of your faith worketh patience. But let patience have her perfect work, that ye may be perfect and entire, wanting nothing." This verse teaches us that when we face hard times, our faith is being tested and strengthened. Through this testing, God builds patience in us, helping us to grow and mature in ways that prepare us for His purpose. Every setback, every struggle, every moment of frustration is a part of God's plan to make us stronger, wiser, and more able to trust in Him. It may be hard to understand why these things happen, but the Bible encourages us not to give up, not to lose hope, because God is with us, working all things together for good. Romans 8:28 promises, "And we know that all things work together for good to them that love God, to them who are the called according to his purpose." This means that even the most difficult situations have a place in God's plan for our lives. He can use everything we face, even our frustrations, to bring about something good. This doesn't mean that setbacks won't hurt or that we won't feel disappointed, but it does mean that these experiences are not wasted. God sees our struggles, and He promises to use them for our benefit and His glory. We see this truth in the life of Joseph in the Old Testament. Despite facing betrayal by his brothers, slavery, and imprisonment, Joseph continued to trust in God's plan. He didn't understand why he was facing so many setbacks, but he believed that God was with him. In Genesis 50:20, Joseph tells his brothers, "But as for you, ye thought evil against me; but God meant it unto good, to bring to pass, as it is this day, to save much people alive." Joseph's story shows us that God can take even the most painful situations and turn them into something good. When we face setbacks, we can remember Joseph's story and hold onto the hope that God has a purpose for our lives, even when we can't see it. We are also encouraged by the words of Jesus, who told His disciples in John 16:33, "These things I have spoken unto you, that in me ye might have peace. In the world ye shall have tribulation: but be of good cheer; I have overcome the world." Jesus knew that we would face hard times, but He also promised us peace and victory. Because of His love and sacrifice, we can face any setback with the assurance that we are not alone, and that God is bigger than any problem we may encounter. The Bible also tells us that our perseverance has eternal value. In 2 Corinthians 4:17-18, we read, "For our light affliction, which is but for a moment, worketh for us a far more exceeding and eternal weight of glory; While we look not at the things which are seen, but at the things which are not seen: for the things which are seen are temporal; but the things which are not seen are eternal." This reminds us that while our struggles may seem overwhelming right now, they are temporary compared to the eternal glory that God has prepared for us. Our perseverance in these trials matters because it brings us closer to the everlasting joy and peace that we will experience with God in heaven. It may be hard to keep this perspective in the middle of frustration, but when we focus on God's promises, we find the strength to keep going. Galatians 6:9 encourages us, "And let us not be weary in well doing: for in due season we shall reap, if we faint not." This verse reminds us that perseverance is key; it is the bridge between planting seeds of faith and seeing the harvest of God's blessings. When we feel like giving up, this verse calls us to hold on, trusting that God will bring us through our struggles and reward our faithfulness. Our setbacks do not define us; rather, our response to them does. When we choose to persevere, we are choosing to believe that God is greater than any obstacle, and that His purpose for us will prevail. Hebrews 12:1-2 encourages us to run with patience, looking to Jesus as our example: "Wherefore seeing we also are compassed about with so great a cloud of witnesses, let us lay aside every weight, and the sin which doth so easily beset us, and let us run with patience the race that is set before us, Looking unto Jesus the author and finisher of our faith; who for the joy that was set before him endured the cross, despising the shame, and is set down at the right hand of the throne of God." Jesus endured unimaginable suffering for our sake, yet He didn't give up. His example reminds us that our perseverance matters because it is a way of following Him, of honoring His sacrifice, and of becoming more like Him. When we look to Jesus, we find the courage to keep going, even when the path is difficult. The Bible also shows us that God gives us the strength to endure. Isaiah 40:31 promises, "But they that wait upon the Lord shall renew their strength; they shall mount up with wings as eagles; they shall run, and not be weary; and they shall walk, and not faint." God doesn't leave us to face our setbacks alone; He gives us the strength we need to persevere. When we feel weak, when frustration is overwhelming, we can turn to God, trusting that He will renew our strength and help us to keep going. We may not always understand why we are facing certain challenges, but we can trust that God is with us and that He will see us through. Perseverance matters because it is a testament to our faith, a declaration that we believe in God's promises and His power to turn every setback into a stepping stone. Each time we choose to keep going, even in the face of disappointment, we are declaring that we trust God's plan, that we believe He is working for our good, and that we know He has a purpose for our lives. Romans 5:3-5 reminds us of this hope: "And not only so, but we glory in tribulations also: knowing that tribulation worketh patience; And patience, experience; and experience, hope: And hope maketh not ashamed; because the love of God is shed abroad in our hearts by the Holy Ghost which is given unto us." This passage shows us that our trials produce patience, which in turn builds experience and hope. When we face setbacks with perseverance, we are not only growing stronger in our faith but also drawing closer to God, who fills our hearts with His love and gives us the hope to keep moving forward. So, why does it matter to persevere in the face of setbacks? It matters because each act of perseverance brings us closer to God, strengthens our faith, and prepares us for the blessings He has in store. It matters because through perseverance, we find hope, a hope that is rooted in

God's promises and His unfailing love. This hope keeps us going, even in the darkest times, reminding us that God is with us, that He is for us, and that He will never leave us. Perseverance is not just about getting through tough times; it is about becoming more like Christ, who endured the cross for the joy that was set before Him. It is about holding onto the truth that God is working all things together for our good, even when we can't see it. And it is about trusting that every setback is a part of God's plan, a stepping stone to the greater purpose He has for our lives.

Day 2 - Purpose Beyond the Pain

In life, pain is something we all experience, and it often leaves us questioning why we have to go through it, especially when it feels like it serves no purpose. It's easy to feel lost in these moments, wondering if there's any reason behind our suffering, any hope beyond the pain. But from a Biblical perspective, pain isn't pointless; it has a purpose, and God often uses our hardest moments to shape us in ways we might not understand. When we look to the Bible, we see that pain and hardship are parts of the journey, and they serve to grow us, mold us, and bring us closer to God. One of the most comforting promises is in Romans 8:28, which says, "And we know that all things work together for good to them that love God, to them who are the called according to his purpose." This verse reminds us that even though pain might feel overwhelming and meaningless, God is weaving everything together for a purpose beyond what we can see. It's a promise that, while we might not understand why we're suffering, God sees the full picture and has a purpose for each moment. In our times of frustration and pain, we can trust that He is working something good out of what seems bad. This promise doesn't take the pain away, but it gives us hope, reminding us that God never wastes our struggles. Just as gold is refined through fire, God uses our trials to refine us. James 1:2-4 speaks to this, saying, "My brethren, count it all joy when ye fall into divers temptations; Knowing this, that the trying of your faith worketh patience. But let patience have her perfect work, that ye may be perfect and entire, wanting nothing." The idea of counting pain as joy can seem confusing, but it points to the truth that pain has a purpose: it builds endurance, patience, and strength in us. God is using each trial to make us more complete, stronger in faith, and closer to Him. Through pain, we learn to rely on God in a deeper way, to trust Him beyond what we can understand. Pain forces us to look beyond ourselves and turn to God for comfort, guidance, and strength. In moments of frustration, it's easy to feel abandoned, but God promises to be with us through it all. In Psalm 34:18, we read, "The Lord is nigh unto them that are of a broken heart; and saveth such as be of a contrite spirit." This verse reminds us that God is especially close to us when we are brokenhearted. Our pain draws God near, and He becomes our source of comfort and healing. Knowing that God is with us in our pain can give us the strength to keep going, to keep hoping, and to believe that there is purpose even in the darkest times. We see this in the life of Joseph, who faced betrayal, slavery, and imprisonment, yet through it all, he trusted in God's plan. In Genesis 50:20, he tells his brothers, "But as for you, ye thought evil against me; but God meant it unto good, to bring to pass, as it is this day, to save much people alive." Joseph's story shows us that God can take even the worst situations and use them for a greater purpose. His pain was not wasted; it was used to fulfill God's plan not only for him but for others. Our pain, too, can serve a purpose beyond ourselves, often becoming a way God works through us to help others, to bring comfort, and to show His power. When we remember that God can use our pain for good, it gives us a reason to hold onto hope, to believe that there is something beyond the hurt we feel now. The Bible also shows us that Jesus Himself understood pain on a profound level. Isaiah 53:3-5 describes Him as "a man of sorrows, and acquainted with grief," who was "wounded for our transgressions" and "bruised for our iniquities." Jesus experienced pain so deep that He cried out to God, asking if the cup of suffering could pass from Him. Yet, He endured it all for a purpose beyond Himself—He endured so that we could be saved, forgiven, and given eternal life. His suffering was not in vain, and neither is ours. Jesus' life reminds us that pain can lead to redemption, hope, and victory. Through His example, we learn that there is purpose in our suffering, even when we can't see it, and that God can bring beauty from ashes, joy from mourning, and strength from weakness. Our pain may sometimes feel pointless, but through faith, we can trust that God is working in ways beyond our understanding. In 2 Corinthians 4:17-18, we are encouraged with these words: "For our light affliction, which is but for a moment, worketh for us a far more exceeding and eternal weight of glory; While we look not at the things which are seen, but at the things which are not seen: for the things which are seen are temporal; but the things which are not seen are eternal." This verse reminds us that our struggles are temporary, but the growth, the character, and the faith they build are eternal. There is a purpose beyond the pain, and it leads to something lasting and beautiful in God's eyes. Pain reminds us that this world is not our final home; it causes us to look to eternity and to long for the day when God will wipe away every tear and make all things new. Revelation 21:4 offers a glimpse of this hope, saying, "And God shall wipe away all tears from their eyes; and there shall be no more death, neither sorrow, nor crying, neither shall there be any more pain: for the former things are passed away." This promise gives us hope that one day, pain will end, and we will be with God in a place of eternal joy and peace. Until then, our pain serves a purpose, drawing us closer to God, shaping us, and reminding us of the hope we have in Him. It matters to find purpose beyond the pain because it strengthens our faith, gives us hope, and helps us persevere. Romans 5:3-5 echoes this truth, saying, "And not only so, but we glory in tribulations also: knowing that tribulation worketh patience; And patience, experience; and experience, hope: And hope maketh not ashamed; because the love of God is shed abroad in our hearts by the Holy Ghost which is given unto us." Pain produces endurance, which builds character and strengthens our hope, and this hope does not disappoint because it is rooted in God's love. Each moment of pain is a step toward becoming more like Christ, toward knowing God more deeply, and toward experiencing His love more fully. Our pain matters because it brings us closer to God, and through it, we find a deeper purpose, a reason to keep believing, and a hope that goes beyond what we can see.

Day 3 - Patience When Progress is Slow

IN LIFE, WE OFTEN WANT things to happen quickly, especially when we work hard or pray earnestly, hoping to see progress and change. Yet, there are times when progress feels painfully slow, and frustration sets in as we wonder if our efforts even matter. In these moments, we may feel discouraged, questioning if we're on the right path or if God is listening to our prayers. The

Bible speaks to this struggle, showing us why patience is essential when progress seems slow and why God sometimes allows us to wait. Patience, especially in times of waiting, is a fruit of the Spirit, something God wants to cultivate in us because it makes us stronger and draws us closer to Him. In Galatians 5:22-23, we read that patience, or "longsuffering," is a quality that reflects God's character. When we practice patience, we are becoming more like Him, learning to trust His timing rather than insisting on our own. Proverbs 3:5-6 reminds us, "Trust in the Lord with all thine heart; and lean not unto thine own understanding. In all thy ways acknowledge him, and he shall direct thy paths." This means that even when we can't see immediate results, we are called to trust that God's ways are better than our own. Patience matters because it teaches us to rely on God, to put our faith in His plan, even when it doesn't make sense to us. It's easy to trust God when things are going well, but true faith is shown in seasons of waiting, in moments when progress is slow and we feel tempted to give up. The Bible assures us that waiting is not wasted time. Isaiah 40:31 says, "But they that wait upon the Lord shall renew their strength; they shall mount up with wings as eagles; they shall run, and not be weary; and they shall walk, and not faint." This verse encourages us that waiting on God isn't passive; it's an active faith that renews our strength. When we wait on the Lord, He gives us what we need to keep going, even when progress is slow. Waiting with patience allows us to develop a deeper strength, one that can't be shaken by the ups and downs of life. Each day we wait is a day we grow in faith, learning to trust that God's timing is perfect and that He knows exactly when to bring His plans to fulfillment. God has a purpose for every delay, even if we can't see it at the time. In Ecclesiastes 3:1, we are reminded, "To every thing there is a season, and a time to every purpose under the heaven." This verse teaches us that life operates on God's timeline, not ours. There is a season for every purpose, and sometimes that purpose requires us to wait. God sees the whole picture when we only see a small part. Just like a farmer plants seeds and waits patiently for the harvest, we must trust that God is working beneath the surface, preparing something beautiful even if it takes time to see it. James 5:7-8 encourages us with this same idea, saying, "Behold, the husbandman waiteth for the precious fruit of the earth, and hath long patience for it, until he receive the early and latter rain. Be ye also patient; stablish your hearts: for the coming of the Lord draweth nigh." This passage shows us that patience is like a farmer waiting for crops to grow; he can't rush the process, but he knows that the harvest will come in its due time. In the same way, we are called to be patient and steady, knowing that God's promises are sure. Waiting is a time of preparation, a season where God is working in us, developing our character and strengthening our faith. Through patience, we learn endurance, which helps us handle the blessings God has for us. In Romans 5:3-4, we read, "And not only so, but we glory in tribulations also: knowing that tribulation worketh patience; And patience, experience; and experience, hope." This shows us that patience builds experience, and experience builds hope. Each time we wait, we gain more strength, more wisdom, and more hope. When progress is slow, God is using the waiting to make us more complete, helping us to grow into the people He created us to be. Patience teaches us humility, reminding us that we are not in control, but that God is. It helps us to let go of our need to rush things and allows us to trust in His perfect timing. In our world today, we are used to getting things quickly, but God's ways are different. In Psalm 37:7, we are encouraged to "Rest in the Lord, and wait patiently for him." Patience matters because it helps us rest in God, letting go of our need to control and trusting that He is at work. This rest gives us peace, even when we don't see immediate results. We don't have to strive or force things to happen; instead, we can find peace in knowing that God is taking care of every detail, and He knows exactly what He's doing. Jesus also understood the importance of patience, as He often used parables to show how God's kingdom works in ways that require time and growth. In Mark 4:26-29, He told the parable of the growing seed, saying, "So is the kingdom of God, as if a man should cast seed into the ground; And should sleep, and rise night and day, and the seed should spring and grow up, he knoweth not how." This parable reminds us that spiritual growth, like physical growth, takes time, and much of it happens unseen. Patience allows us to trust that God is working even when we can't see immediate results. Waiting on God's timing can be difficult, but it strengthens our faith and brings us closer to Him. Psalm 27:14 encourages us, "Wait on the Lord: be of good courage, and he shall strengthen thine heart: wait, I say, on the Lord." When we wait with courage and patience, God strengthens us, giving us the ability to keep going even when progress is slow. He is using each moment to teach us to rely on Him more fully, to grow in faith, and to become people of endurance. Patience matters because it changes us from the inside, making us more like

Christ. Jesus waited for the right time to begin His ministry, waited for God's timing in every decision, and showed patience even in the face of suffering. Hebrews 12:2 tells us, "Looking unto Jesus the author and finisher of our faith; who for the joy that was set before him endured the cross, despising the shame, and is set down at the right hand of the throne of God." Jesus endured with patience, knowing that God's plan would be fulfilled in the right time. His example reminds us that patience is not about giving up but about trusting that God's timing is perfect. When progress is slow, we can look to Jesus as our example, knowing that He walked this path of patience before us. We also find hope in knowing that God has a purpose for our lives, and His timing is always right. Jeremiah 29:11 reminds us, "For I know the thoughts that I think toward you, saith the Lord, thoughts of peace, and not of evil, to give you an expected end." God's plans are good, and even when it feels like we're waiting too long, we can trust that He is leading us to a place of peace and blessing. Patience helps us to hold on to this hope, to keep trusting even when progress is slow. It matters because it builds our faith, strengthens our relationship with God, and prepares us for the blessings He has in store. In moments of frustration, when progress feels slow, we are called to hold onto this truth, to let patience have its perfect work in us, knowing that God is faithful and His timing is always right.

Day 4 - Pushing Through the Pressure

In life, we all face pressures that can feel overwhelming, moments that make us want to give up and wonder why we should keep going. These pressures can come from many places—school, work, relationships, health, or just the weight of life itself—and they often make us feel like there's no way out. Yet, the Bible teaches us that pushing through pressure is not only possible, but it's also an important part of our journey with God. The Bible gives us hope and guidance, showing us why it matters to keep going, to trust God even when the weight of life feels too heavy to carry. Pushing through pressure builds our faith, brings us closer to God, and shows us that we are not alone, for God is with us every step of the way. In 2 Corinthians 4:8-9, we read, "We are troubled on every side, yet not distressed; we are perplexed, but not in despair; Persecuted, but not forsaken; cast down, but not destroyed." This powerful message reminds us that even when we feel pressed on all sides, God does not abandon us. We may feel troubled and pressured, but we are not crushed, because God is holding us up, giving us the strength to keep going. When life feels like it's closing in, these verses remind us that God is our hope, our refuge, and our reason to keep pushing forward, knowing that He has a purpose even for our struggles.

One of the hardest parts of facing pressure is feeling like we have to bear it all on our own. But in Matthew 11:28-30, Jesus invites us to come to Him with our burdens, saying, "Come unto me, all ye that labour and are heavy laden, and I will give you rest. Take my yoke upon you, and learn of me; for I am meek and lowly in heart: and ye shall find rest unto your souls. For my yoke is easy, and my burden is light." This invitation from Jesus reminds us that we don't have to face life's pressures alone. He is there to help carry our burdens, to walk beside us, and to give us the rest we need when we feel weary. When the pressures of life feel too heavy, Jesus calls us to bring them to Him, to trust that He is strong enough to carry what we cannot. His promise gives us hope and strength to keep pushing through, knowing that we are not alone in our struggles.

The Bible also teaches us that pressure is not pointless; it has a purpose in our lives. Romans 5:3-4 tells us, "And not only so, but we glory in tribulations also: knowing that tribulation worketh patience; And patience, experience; and experience, hope." This verse shows us that God uses pressure to build patience in us, to help us grow stronger and more resilient. Each time we push through a hard moment, we are gaining experience and learning to trust God more deeply. This experience gives us hope, a hope that is not based on our own strength but on God's faithfulness. When we face pressure with patience and perseverance, we are learning to depend on God and to see that He is with us in every challenge. The strength that comes from pushing through pressure is a strength that can only come from God, a strength that helps us keep going even when life feels overwhelming.

In James 1:12, we are given another encouragement: "Blessed is the man that endureth temptation: for when he is tried, he shall receive the crown of life, which the Lord hath promised to them that love him." This verse reminds us that those who endure pressure and remain faithful will be blessed by God. Our struggles are not for nothing; God sees every effort we make to stay faithful, every tear we shed, and every moment we feel overwhelmed. When we push through, we are working toward something greater than ourselves, a reward that God has promised. Pushing through pressure, even when it's hard, is a way of showing our love for God and our trust in His promises. It reminds us that our trials are temporary, but the blessings that God has prepared for us are eternal.

One of the most comforting truths about pushing through pressure is knowing that God understands our struggles. Hebrews 4:15 reminds us, "For we have not an high priest which cannot be touched with the feeling of our infirmities; but was in all points tempted like as we are, yet without sin." Jesus faced pressure, temptation, and hardship, and He knows exactly what it feels like to be overwhelmed. He walked this path before us, and He overcame. Because of this, we can trust that Jesus is with us, that He understands our pain, and that He will help us to push through. In moments of pressure, we can turn to Jesus, knowing that He has been where we are and that He overcame for our sake. This truth gives us hope, a reason to keep going, and the strength to push forward even when life feels impossible.

Psalm 46:1 tells us, "God is our refuge and strength, a very present help in trouble." This verse reminds us that God is not distant; He is with us, ready to help us in our hardest moments. When we feel the weight of pressure pressing down, we can find refuge in God, a safe place where we are held, loved, and supported. Pushing through pressure with God's help reminds us that we are not defined by our struggles; we are defined by God's love and His strength within us. His presence gives us the courage to keep going, to face each day with hope, and to believe that we will come out stronger on the other side.

Isaiah 41:10 offers us this encouragement: "Fear thou not; for I am with thee: be not dismayed; for I am thy God: I will strengthen thee; yea, I will help thee; yea, I will uphold thee with the right hand of my righteousness." This verse is a reminder that we don't have to be afraid of pressure, because God is with us. He promises to strengthen us, to help us, and to uphold us when we feel weak. When we push through pressure, we are leaning on God's strength, trusting that He will carry us when we cannot carry ourselves. His promise to be with us gives us the courage to keep going, knowing that we are held by His righteous hand.

Finally, we see in Philippians 4:13 a powerful truth that helps us push through any pressure: "I can do all things through Christ which strengtheneth me." This verse is a reminder that with Christ, we are capable of facing any challenge, enduring any pressure, and overcoming any obstacle. It's not by our own strength but by Christ's power within us that we are able to keep going. When the weight of pressure feels too heavy, we can remember that Christ is our strength, that He empowers us to do what seems impossible. Pushing through pressure matters because it is a testimony of God's strength in our lives, a reminder that with Him, we can face anything.

In moments of pressure, we have the choice to give up or to lean into God's promises. When we choose to push through, we are choosing to trust that God has a purpose for our struggles, that He is with us, and that He will bring us through to the other side. Pushing through pressure matters because it is an act of faith, a declaration that we believe in God's power, His presence, and His promises. Each time we push through, we are becoming stronger, not in our own strength, but in the strength that comes from trusting in God. We are growing, learning, and becoming more like Christ. Through every pressure we face, we are reminded that God is our refuge, our strength, and our hope, and that with Him, we are never alone.

Day 5 - Peace in the Midst of Uncertainty

In life, we all go through seasons of uncertainty, times when the future feels unclear, and we're not sure what will happen next. This uncertainty can create a deep sense of frustration, confusion, and even fear. We wonder why things aren't working out the way we planned and why answers seem so far away. In these moments, it's easy to feel overwhelmed, but the Bible offers us a powerful truth: that we can find peace even in the midst of uncertainty. God's Word teaches us that He is with us, guiding us, comforting us, and giving us strength, even when we can't see the road ahead. In John 14:27, Jesus tells us, "Peace I leave with you, my peace I give unto you: not as the world giveth, give I unto you. Let not your heart be troubled, neither let it be afraid." This promise from Jesus reminds us that the peace He offers is unlike any peace the world can give; it is a deep, lasting peace that comes from knowing He is in control. When we feel like life is spinning out of control, this peace becomes our anchor, holding us steady, reminding us that we are not alone and that God has a plan, even if we cannot yet see it.

One of the hardest parts of facing uncertainty is the feeling that we are waiting without answers, not knowing which way to go. Proverbs 3:5-6 encourages us, "Trust in the Lord with all thine heart; and lean not unto thine own understanding. In all thy ways acknowledge him, and he shall direct thy paths." This verse reminds us that we don't have to understand everything; instead, we are called to trust God fully. When we lean on Him rather than our own understanding, we allow Him to guide us, to lead us step by step. This trust is what brings peace, knowing that God sees the whole picture, even when we can only see a small part. As we trust in God's wisdom, He directs our paths, leading us in ways that are often better than anything we could have planned. Trusting in God during uncertain times can feel difficult, but it's also freeing because it means we don't have to figure everything out on our own. We can rest in the knowledge that God is faithful, that He knows what we need, and that He will guide us through.

In Philippians 4:6-7, we find another powerful reminder about finding peace: "Be careful for nothing; but in every thing by prayer and supplication with thanksgiving let your requests be made known unto God. And the peace of God, which passeth all understanding, shall keep your hearts and minds through Christ Jesus." Here, we are encouraged to bring our worries and frustrations to God in prayer, to open our hearts to Him and trust that He is listening. When we pray and lay our burdens at God's feet, we receive His peace, a peace that goes beyond what we can understand. This peace guards our hearts and minds, keeping us calm even when life feels uncertain. Prayer is not just about asking God for what we need; it's about connecting with Him, spending time in His presence, and allowing His peace to fill us. In prayer, we are reminded that God is near, that He cares deeply for us, and that He is working in ways we cannot see.

Psalm 46:10 encourages us to "Be still, and know that I am God." In times of uncertainty, this verse reminds us that we don't have to rush or force things to happen. Instead, we are called to be still, to rest in God's presence, and to remember that He is in control. Being still means letting go of our worries and trusting that God's timing is perfect. It's in this stillness that we find peace, knowing that God is with us, that He sees every detail of our lives, and that He is working things out for our good. When we let go and trust God, we open ourselves to His peace, a peace that holds us steady no matter what happens.

One of the greatest comforts in times of uncertainty is knowing that God's plans for us are good. Jeremiah 29:11 reminds us, "For I know the thoughts that I think toward you, saith the Lord, thoughts of peace, and not of evil, to give you an expected end." God's plans are filled with peace and hope, and He has a purpose for each of us. When we feel uncertain about the future, we can hold onto this promise, trusting that God's plans are good and that He will lead us to a place of peace. Even when we don't understand why things are happening the way they are, we can find hope in knowing that God is in control and that He has a future filled with hope and purpose for us. This hope gives us peace, a deep assurance that we are in God's hands, no matter what uncertainties we face.

Isaiah 26:3 also speaks of this peace, saying, "Thou wilt keep him in perfect peace, whose mind is stayed on thee: because he trusteth in thee." This verse shows us that peace comes from focusing on God rather than our problems. When we fix our minds on God, when we think about His goodness, His faithfulness, and His promises, we find peace. Trusting in God keeps us from being overwhelmed by uncertainty because our focus shifts from what we don't know to the One who knows everything. God promises to keep us in perfect peace if we keep our minds on Him, and this peace is what helps us face each day with calm and confidence, knowing that we are not alone.

Jesus also offers comfort in Matthew 6:34, saying, "Take therefore no thought for the morrow: for the morrow shall take thought for the things of itself. Sufficient unto the day is the evil thereof." This verse encourages us not to worry about tomorrow but to focus on today, trusting that God will provide what we need each day. Uncertainty about the future can make us anxious, but Jesus reminds us that God will take care of each day as it comes. We don't have to carry the weight of tomorrow's problems today; instead, we can trust that God will give us strength and peace for whatever lies ahead. Focusing on today and trusting God for tomorrow allows us to find peace, knowing that God's provision is constant and that He will never leave us.

Psalm 23:4 also gives us hope in times of uncertainty: "Yea, though I walk through the valley of the shadow of death, I will fear no evil: for thou art with me; thy rod and thy staff they comfort me." This verse reminds us that even in our darkest moments, even when we walk through valleys of fear and uncertainty, God is with us. His presence gives us comfort and courage, helping us to push through the unknown with peace in our hearts. Knowing that God is our shepherd, guiding and protecting us, brings a peace that nothing in this world can offer. No matter how uncertain the path may seem, we are never alone, for God is walking beside us every step of the way.

Finally, Romans 8:28 offers us a powerful truth to hold onto: "And we know that all things work together for good to them that love God, to them who are the called according to his purpose." This verse reminds us that God is able to use every situation, even the uncertain and challenging ones, for our good. Nothing in our lives is wasted; God can bring good out of every difficulty. When we face uncertainty, we can find peace in knowing that God is in control, that He is working behind the scenes, and that His plan will ultimately bring good into our lives. This promise gives us hope and reassurance, helping us to face uncertain times with confidence and peace.

Finding peace in the midst of uncertainty matters because it allows us to live with hope and trust, even when life doesn't make sense. It reminds us that God is greater than any situation, that His love is unchanging, and that His promises are true. Peace doesn't mean everything is perfect; it means we trust

God's plan and His presence in our lives. In moments of frustration, when the future feels unclear, we can hold onto this peace, knowing that God is with us, guiding us, and carrying us through. This peace allows us to face each day with strength, to keep going even when we don't have all the answers, and to rest in the assurance that God is our refuge, our hope, and our constant source of peace.

Day 6 - Persistence When Hope Feels Thin

IN LIFE, THERE ARE times when hope feels thin, when it seems like no matter how hard we try, nothing changes, and we start to feel weary, even defeated. Moments of frustration, disappointment, and loss can make us question if our efforts are worth it and if God even hears our cries. Yet, the Bible reminds us over and over that it's in these times—when hope feels faint—that persistence matters the most. God calls us to keep going, to hold onto faith even when it feels like we're holding on by a thread, because He has a purpose for our perseverance. In Galatians 6:9, we're encouraged with these words: "And let us not be weary in well doing: for in due season we shall reap, if we faint not." This verse is a powerful reminder that even when we feel like giving up, our efforts are not in vain. God sees every prayer we've prayed, every tear we've shed, and every moment we've kept the faith despite feeling discouraged. Persistence matters because it's a declaration of our trust in God, even when circumstances don't seem to be in our favor. When we keep going, we're showing that we believe in God's timing, that we trust His plan even when it's hidden from us. This kind of persistence builds our character and draws us closer to God, helping us grow in faith and resilience.

One of the hardest parts of holding onto hope is the feeling that our efforts are going unnoticed or unanswered. But Hebrews 10:23 reminds us, "Let us hold fast the profession of our faith without wavering; (for he is faithful that promised)." This verse encourages us to cling to our faith, not because everything is going well, but because God is faithful. He doesn't abandon us when things get tough. His promises remain true, and He is working behind the scenes, even when we can't see it. Persistence in these moments is about trusting in God's faithfulness, believing that He will fulfill His promises in His perfect timing. Each time we choose to keep going, we are holding onto that faith, declaring that we believe God is greater than our circumstances. The Bible shows us that God often works in ways that are not immediately visible, like seeds planted deep in the soil. It takes time for growth to show, but the work is happening below the surface. In our own lives, God is often working in unseen ways, building something in us or for us that will bear fruit in time. When we persist, we are allowing God the time and space to work in us and through us, trusting that His timing is better than our own.

Romans 5:3-4 reminds us of the purpose behind our struggles, saying, "And not only so, but we glory in tribulations also: knowing that tribulation worketh patience; And patience, experience; and experience, hope." This passage shows us that challenges and setbacks are not pointless; they are part of a process that leads us to a deeper, more resilient hope. Persistence, especially when hope feels thin, builds patience in us. It teaches us to wait on God, to trust Him more deeply, and to believe that He is always at work. Each trial, each moment of frustration, is an opportunity for God to strengthen our faith. It's not easy to keep going when we're discouraged, but each step we take, each time we choose faith over despair, we are building a stronger foundation in God. Persistence through hardship shapes us, teaching us to rely on God's strength instead of our own, and drawing us closer to Him in ways that only struggle can.

The Bible also shows us examples of those who held onto hope even when their situation seemed hopeless. One of the most powerful examples is the story of Job, a man who lost everything—his family, his health, his wealth—and yet continued to trust in God. In Job 13:15, he declares, "Though he slay me, yet will I trust in him." Job's persistence, even in his darkest moments, shows us that true faith holds on, even when the reason to hope seems thin. Job's story reminds us that our relationship with God is not based on what we receive from Him, but on who He is. Persistence is a way of saying, "I trust You, God, even when I don't understand what You're doing." This kind of faith moves God's heart, and it brings us closer to Him, giving us the strength to endure even the toughest situations.

When hope feels thin, persistence can feel like a daily battle, but it's one worth fighting. James 1:12 encourages us with these words: "Blessed is the man that endureth temptation: for when he is tried, he shall receive the crown of life, which the Lord hath promised to them that love him." This promise reminds us that there is a reward for those who keep going, for those who hold onto their faith in the midst of trials. God sees our persistence, and He honors it. Each time we choose to keep going, we are storing up treasures in heaven, building a legacy of faith that will not be forgotten. Persistence matters because it is an act of faith, a declaration that we believe God is good, that He is faithful, and that He will fulfill His promises, even if we can't see how or when. Holding onto hope when it feels thin is about trusting that God's timing is perfect, that He knows what we need, and that He will bring us through.

Isaiah 40:31 also gives us hope, saying, "But they that wait upon the Lord shall renew their strength; they shall mount up with wings as eagles; they shall run, and not be weary; and they shall walk, and not faint." This verse is a powerful reminder that waiting on God, holding onto hope, and persisting in faith will give us new strength. God promises to renew our strength when we feel weary, to lift us up and help us continue, even when we feel like giving up. Persistence allows us to tap into God's strength rather than relying on our own. It's an invitation to lean on Him, to trust that He will carry us through, and to believe that He is with us in every moment of struggle.

Finally, Romans 8:28 reminds us why persistence matters in the grand scheme of God's plan: "And we know that all things work together for good to them that love God, to them who are the called according to his purpose." This verse assures us that God is able to use every situation, every trial, and every moment of frustration for good. Even when hope feels thin, even when we can't see the good in our circumstances, we can trust that God is working things together for our benefit. Persistence is about holding onto that promise, believing that God's purpose is greater than our understanding, and trusting that He will bring good out of even the hardest moments. When we hold onto hope and keep going, we are aligning ourselves with God's plan, allowing Him to work in our lives in ways we may not yet understand.

In moments of frustration, when hope feels thin, persistence becomes a powerful act of faith. It's a way of saying, "I believe in You, God, even when I can't see the way forward." This kind of persistence deepens our faith, strengthens our character, and brings us closer to God. It reminds us that our hope is not based on our circumstances but on God's unchanging love and His promises. When we choose to keep going, even when it's hard, we are building a foundation of faith that will carry us through any storm. Persistence matters because it helps us grow, it brings us closer to God, and it reminds us that we are never alone. God is with us in every step, giving us the strength to endure, the faith to believe, and the hope to keep moving forward.

Day 7- Perspective on Purposeful Struggles

Life is filled with struggles, and at times it can be hard to understand why we have to face so many challenges and hardships. It's easy to feel frustrated, discouraged, and even defeated when we face one struggle after another, especially when it seems like our efforts aren't bringing any relief or change. But the Bible teaches us that struggles are not just random or meaningless events; they have a purpose, and God can use them to shape and strengthen us in ways that might not be immediately visible. When we look at our struggles from God's perspective, we begin to see that every hardship can serve a greater purpose in our lives, even if we can't fully understand it at the moment. Romans 8:28 reminds us, "And we know that all things work together for good to them that love God, to them who are the called according to his purpose." This verse tells us that God can use every struggle, every trial, and every hardship for good. It doesn't mean that our struggles aren't painful or that we shouldn't feel the weight of them, but it does mean that God is working behind the scenes, taking even the hardest moments and turning them into something that benefits us in the long run. When we trust in God's purpose, we can begin to see our struggles in a different light, recognizing that they are not punishments but opportunities for growth and transformation.

One of the most profound truths about purposeful struggles is that they refine our character. In James 1:2-4, we are encouraged, "My brethren, count it all joy when ye fall into divers temptations; Knowing this, that the trying of your faith worketh patience. But let patience have her perfect work, that ye may be perfect and entire, wanting nothing." This passage reminds us that struggles build patience and endurance within us. Each time we face a challenge and continue to trust in God, we are growing stronger, learning to rely on Him rather than on our own understanding. Struggles are like a refining fire that burns away our doubts, fears, and weaknesses, leaving us with a stronger, purer faith. While it can be hard to find joy in the midst of hardship, this verse encourages us to look beyond the immediate pain and see the growth that is taking place within us. With each struggle, we are being shaped more into the person God created us to be, more resilient, more patient, and more faithful.

The Bible also shows us that struggles draw us closer to God, deepening our relationship with Him. In times of ease, it's easy to rely on ourselves and forget our need for God. But in moments of struggle, we are reminded of our dependence on Him. Psalm 34:18 offers comfort, saying, "The Lord is nigh unto them that are of a broken heart; and saveth such as be of a contrite spirit." This verse tells us that God is close to us in our hardest moments. When we are brokenhearted and struggling, God draws near, offering us His presence, comfort, and strength. Struggles remind us that we are not alone; they teach us to seek God more earnestly and to rely on His strength rather than our own. Through our struggles, we experience God's love and faithfulness in a deeper way, learning to trust Him more fully. It's in these hard moments that we come to know God as our refuge and strength, our source of hope and comfort.

Another purpose of struggles is that they prepare us to help others. In 2 Corinthians 1:3-4, Paul writes, "Blessed be God, even the Father of our Lord Jesus Christ, the Father of mercies, and the God of all comfort; Who comforteth us in all our tribulation, that we may be able to comfort them which are in any trouble, by the comfort wherewith we ourselves are comforted of God." This passage reminds us that our struggles are not just about us; they equip us to be a source of comfort and encouragement to others who may be going through similar situations. When we face hardship and experience God's comfort, we are given the strength and empathy to reach out to others who are hurting. Our struggles give us the ability to speak words of encouragement, to offer compassion, and to point others to the hope we have found in God. Purposeful struggles create a deeper compassion within us, teaching us to be more understanding, patient, and kind to those who are also in need.

Struggles also teach us to value what truly matters and to keep our focus on God's eternal promises rather than on temporary things. In 2 Corinthians 4:17-18, we read, "For our light affliction, which is but for a moment, worketh for us a far more exceeding and eternal weight of glory; While we look not at the things which are seen, but at the things which are not seen: for the things which are seen are temporal; but the things which are not seen are eternal." This passage reminds us that our struggles, though difficult, are temporary compared to the eternal life that awaits us. Struggles teach us to look beyond the here and now, to focus on the things that last forever—our relationship with God, our faith, and our character. When we see our struggles from an eternal perspective, we begin to understand that they are small in comparison to the glory and joy that await us in God's presence. Struggles remind us to hold onto hope, knowing that our present hardships are only a part of our journey, and that God has prepared something far greater for us in eternity.

Jesus Himself experienced struggles and hardships, showing us that even the Son of God was not exempt from suffering. In Hebrews 5:8, we are reminded, "Though he were a Son, yet learned he obedience by the things which he suffered." Jesus faced immense struggles, from temptation in the wilderness to the agony of the cross, yet He persisted and remained faithful to God's purpose. His life shows us that struggles can lead to growth and obedience, drawing us closer to God's will. Jesus' struggles were not in vain; through them, He fulfilled God's purpose and brought salvation to humanity. His example encourages us to persevere, knowing that our struggles, too, can serve a greater purpose.

Struggles, though difficult, can also strengthen our hope. In Romans 5:3-5, Paul writes, "And not only so, but we glory in tribulations also: knowing that tribulation worketh patience; And patience, experience; and experience, hope: And hope maketh not ashamed; because the love of God is shed abroad in our hearts by the Holy Ghost which is given unto us." This passage shows us that struggles are part of a process that leads to a stronger, unshakeable hope. Each time we face hardship and hold onto our faith, we are building a hope that will not disappoint. This hope is grounded in God's love, a love that is with us through every trial and that assures us we are never alone. Struggles teach us to look to God, to trust in His love, and to believe in His promises, knowing that He is faithful and that He will see us through.

Ultimately, seeing our struggles as purposeful helps us to keep going, to persevere, and to find hope even when things feel overwhelming. Our struggles are not the end of our story; they are part of a greater plan that God has for us. We may not always understand why we are facing certain hardships, but we can trust that God knows what He is doing. Jeremiah 29:11 reminds us, "For I know the thoughts that I think toward you, saith the Lord, thoughts of peace, and not of evil, to give you an expected end." God's plans for us are filled with hope and purpose, and He promises to use every struggle, every hardship, and every trial for our good. When we hold onto this perspective, we find the strength to keep going, to trust that God is working in ways we cannot see, and to believe that our struggles are shaping us for something greater.

Day 8 - Power in Staying the Course

In life, we all face moments when the road ahead feels long and difficult, when it seems easier to give up than to keep going. Frustration, disappointment, and hardship can make us feel weary, making us question if it's worth staying the course, especially when progress feels slow or invisible. Yet, the Bible teaches us that there is great power in staying the course, even when we feel like giving up. God calls us to persevere, to keep going even when it's hard, because He has a purpose for every step we take. In Galatians 6:9, we are encouraged, "And let us not be weary in well doing: for in due season we shall reap, if we faint not." This verse reminds us that our efforts are not in vain; there is a reward for those who hold on, who trust in God's timing, and who believe that He is at work even when they cannot see it. Staying the course means trusting in God's promises and knowing that He will bring everything to fulfillment in His perfect time. It is in these moments of faithfulness, when we keep going despite our frustrations, that God strengthens us, teaching us to rely on Him and reminding us that He is with us every step of the way.

One of the reasons why it matters to stay the course is because persistence builds our character. In Romans 5:3-4, we read, "And not only so, but we glory in tribulations also: knowing that tribulation worketh patience; And patience, experience; and experience, hope." This verse teaches us that trials and hardships serve a purpose in our lives; they build patience and perseverance. Each time we choose to stay the course, to keep moving forward in faith, we are building a deeper strength within ourselves, a strength that can only come through endurance. Staying the course helps us to develop patience, a quality that teaches us to wait on God's timing and to trust that He knows what is best. When we persist, we are allowing God to shape us, to refine us, and to make us more like Him. The challenges we face along the way are not meant to break us but to build us, to help us grow in faith and in resilience. Staying the course, even when it's hard, is a way of showing God that we trust Him, that we believe He is at work, and that we are willing to keep going because we know He has a purpose for our journey.

The Bible also reminds us that staying the course brings us closer to God. In times of struggle, it's easy to feel like we are alone, but God is always with us, guiding us and strengthening us. In James 4:8, we are encouraged, "Draw nigh to God, and he will draw nigh to you." This verse tells us that as we draw closer to God, He draws closer to us. Staying the course, especially in difficult times, is an opportunity to deepen our relationship with God, to seek His presence, and to rely on His strength. When we feel weak, God becomes our strength; when we feel lost, He becomes our guide. Staying the course helps us to see that we are not alone, that God is with us, walking beside us, helping us carry our burdens. Each step we take in faith is a step closer to God, a step that brings us into a deeper understanding of His love and His faithfulness. Through our struggles, we learn to depend on God more fully, realizing that He is the one who gives us the power to keep going.

Another reason why staying the course matters is because it is a testimony of our faith. In Hebrews 11:1, we read, "Now faith is the substance of things hoped for, the evidence of things not seen." Faith is about believing in what we cannot see, trusting that God is working behind the scenes, even when our circumstances seem bleak. Staying the course is a way of demonstrating that faith, of showing that we believe God's promises are true, even if we cannot see the results yet. Our persistence is a declaration that we trust God's plan, that we believe He is faithful, and that we are willing to keep going because we know He is with us. Each time we choose to stay the course, we are making a statement of faith, a statement that says, "I believe in God's goodness, in His timing, and in His power to bring me through." This kind of faith is powerful, and it encourages others as well, showing them that it is possible to keep going, to trust in God, and to find hope even in the hardest moments.

Staying the course also teaches us to focus on the eternal rather than the temporary. In 2 Corinthians 4:17-18, Paul writes, "For our light affliction, which is but for a moment, worketh for us a far more exceeding and eternal weight of glory; While we look not at the things which are seen, but at the things which are not seen: for the things which are seen are temporal; but the things which are not seen are eternal." This verse reminds us that our struggles, though real and painful, are temporary compared to the eternal rewards that God has prepared for us. Staying the course helps us to keep our eyes on the bigger picture, to remember that this life is not all there is, and that God has something greater in store for us. When we focus on eternity, we find the strength to keep going, knowing that every step we take in faith is bringing us closer to God's promises. Staying the course matters because it shifts our perspective, helping us to see beyond our current struggles and to hold onto the hope of eternal life with God.

One of the greatest examples of staying the course is found in the life of Jesus. In Hebrews 12:2, we are encouraged, "Looking unto Jesus the author and finisher of our faith; who for the joy that was set before him endured the cross, despising the shame, and is set down at the right hand of the throne of God." Jesus faced immense suffering and hardship, yet He stayed the course, enduring the cross because He knew it was part of God's plan. His example shows us that staying the course is not about avoiding hardship but about remaining faithful to God's purpose, even when it's difficult. Jesus' perseverance brought salvation to humanity, and His example encourages us to keep going, to trust that God's plan is greater than our struggles, and to know that there is a purpose for every step we take. When we look to Jesus, we find the strength to stay the course, knowing that He walked this path before us and that He will help us to endure as well.

Finally, staying the course brings honor to God. In Psalm 37:5, we read, "Commit thy way unto the Lord; trust also in him; and he shall bring it to pass." This verse encourages us to commit our path to God, to trust Him, and to believe that He will fulfill His promises. Staying the course is an act of worship, a way of honoring God by showing that we trust His guidance, His wisdom, and His love. When we choose to stay the course, we are saying that we believe in God's ability to bring us through, that we trust Him to lead us, and that we are willing to follow Him, no matter how hard the journey may be. Staying the course is a way of giving God glory, of showing that our faith is in Him and not in our circumstances. It matters because it demonstrates our love and devotion to God, a devotion that is not based on convenience but on commitment.

In moments of frustration, when it feels like giving up would be easier, staying the course becomes a powerful act of faith. It reminds us that we are not alone, that God is with us, and that He is working in ways we cannot see. Staying the course builds our character, strengthens our faith, and brings us closer to God. It shows others that hope is real, that God is faithful, and that there is a purpose for every step we take. When we stay the course, we are choosing to believe in God's goodness, to trust in His timing, and to know that He will bring us through. Staying the course matters because it is a testament to our faith, a declaration that we believe in God's promises, and a commitment to keep going, no matter what challenges we face. In every moment of perseverance, we are honoring God, building our hope, and finding the strength to continue, knowing that God has a plan and that He will be with us every step of the way.

Day 9 - Pathways to Peaceful Resolve

In life, there are many moments when frustration can seem overwhelming, when the struggles we face make peace feel far away and nearly impossible to reach. We try to hold onto faith, but doubts, fears, and hardships make it hard to find a sense of calm and hope in our hearts. Frustration can drain our energy, make us question our purpose, and even distance us from God. Yet, the Bible teaches us that no matter how challenging our path, there are always pathways to a peaceful resolve, ways to find rest and comfort even in the midst of life's storms. God has given us promises that offer hope, encouragement, and peace, guiding us back to Him and reminding us that He is our source of strength. In John 14:27, Jesus tells us, "Peace I leave with you, my peace I give unto you: not as the world giveth, give I unto you. Let not your heart be troubled, neither let it be afraid." This powerful promise reminds us that God's peace is different from anything the world can offer. It is a peace that calms our hearts, a peace that comes from knowing that God is with us, guiding us, and holding us close. No matter how frustrated we feel, this peace is available to us through our faith in Christ, giving us a sense of resolve and strength to face each day, even when the way forward is uncertain.

One of the most important pathways to peaceful resolve is trusting in God's plan and timing. Proverbs 3:5-6 encourages us to "Trust in the Lord with all thine heart; and lean not unto thine own understanding. In all thy ways acknowledge him, and he shall direct thy paths." This verse teaches us that we don't need to have all the answers or understand every detail of our struggles. Instead, we are called to trust in God, to lean on His wisdom, and to believe that He is directing our steps. Trusting in God's plan brings peace because it reminds us that we don't have to figure everything out on our own. God sees the bigger picture, and He knows what we need, even when we are uncertain or fearful. When we let go of our need to control everything and place our trust in God, we find a sense of calm and assurance that He is leading us toward His purpose, even through the frustrations of life.

Prayer is another vital pathway to peace. In Philippians 4:6-7, we are told, "Be careful for nothing; but in every thing by prayer and supplication with thanksgiving let your requests be made known unto God. And the peace of

God, which passeth all understanding, shall keep your hearts and minds through Christ Jesus." When we bring our worries, frustrations, and fears to God in prayer, we open our hearts to His peace. Prayer allows us to lay down our burdens, to release our anxieties, and to connect with God in a personal way. It reminds us that we are not alone and that we can find comfort and guidance in His presence. As we pray, we experience a peace that goes beyond our circumstances, a peace that fills our hearts with hope and strength. Prayer is a reminder that God is near, that He hears us, and that He is working on our behalf, even when we can't see it.

Being still in God's presence is also a pathway to finding peace. Psalm 46:10 tells us, "Be still, and know that I am God." In the busyness of life, it's easy to get caught up in our frustrations, to feel like we have to keep pushing forward even when we're weary. But this verse reminds us that there is power in stillness, in pausing to remember that God is in control. Being still means letting go of our struggles and trusting that God is working, even in ways we can't see. It is in these quiet moments of surrender that we find peace, a peace that comes from knowing that we are held in God's hands. When we take time to be still, we allow God's peace to fill our hearts, to calm our minds, and to remind us that He is with us, guiding us through every challenge.

The Bible also teaches us that focusing on God's promises helps us find peace. In Isaiah 26:3, we read, "Thou wilt keep him in perfect peace, whose mind is stayed on thee: because he trusteth in thee." This verse shows us that peace comes when we fix our thoughts on God, when we remember His faithfulness, His love, and His promises. By keeping our minds focused on God, we are reminded that He is greater than our struggles and that His promises are true. His Word is filled with promises of hope, comfort, and strength, and by meditating on these promises, we find a sense of peace that helps us through even the toughest times. God's promises are a source of comfort, guiding us back to Him and reminding us that He will never leave us or forsake us.

Another pathway to peace is forgiveness. In moments of frustration, it's easy to hold onto anger, resentment, or bitterness, especially when we feel hurt or wronged. But holding onto these feelings only adds to our frustration and steals our peace. In Colossians 3:13, we are encouraged, "Forbearing one another, and forgiving one another, if any man have a quarrel against any: even as Christ forgave you, so also do ye." Forgiveness frees us from the weight of bitterness and allows us to experience God's peace. By forgiving others, we let go of the burdens that keep us trapped in frustration, making space for God's love and peace to fill our hearts. Forgiveness is not always easy, but it is a pathway to peaceful resolve, a way of releasing our hurts and trusting that God will bring healing and justice in His own time.

Gratitude is also a powerful pathway to peace. When we focus on what we lack or what is going wrong, frustration grows. But when we choose to be grateful, even in difficult times, we shift our perspective and find peace in God's blessings. In 1 Thessalonians 5:18, we are reminded, "In every thing give thanks: for this is the will of God in Christ Jesus concerning you." Gratitude helps us to see God's goodness, to remember His faithfulness, and to trust that He is working in our lives. By choosing to be thankful, we open our hearts to peace, a peace that comes from knowing that God is providing for us, caring for us, and walking with us every step of the way. Gratitude reminds us of all the ways God has blessed us, helping us to see beyond our frustrations and find joy in His presence.

Finally, focusing on God's eternal promises gives us a pathway to peace. In 2 Corinthians 4:17-18, we are encouraged, "For our light affliction, which is but for a moment, worketh for us a far more exceeding and eternal weight of glory; While we look not at the things which are seen, but at the things which are not seen: for the things which are seen are temporal; but the things which are not seen are eternal." This verse reminds us that our struggles are temporary compared to the eternal life God has prepared for us. When we focus on God's eternal promises, we find peace in knowing that our current frustrations and hardships are only part of a bigger picture. God has promised us eternal joy, peace, and life with Him, and this hope gives us strength to endure, to trust, and to keep moving forward with faith. By keeping our eyes on eternity, we find peace that helps us through our present struggles, reminding us that God's plan is far greater than we can imagine.

Finding pathways to peaceful resolve is not always easy, especially when frustration is high and hope feels thin. But through prayer, trust, forgiveness, gratitude, and a focus on God's promises, we can experience a peace that carries us through every challenge. This peace is a gift from God, a reminder that we are not alone, that He is with us, and that He is working for our good. Each time we turn to Him, we find a pathway to peace, a way of resting in His love and finding strength in His promises. No matter how tough the road may be, God offers us His peace, guiding us to a place of resolve, comfort, and hope. In His presence, we find the peace we need to keep going, to face each day with faith, and to know that He will see us through every trial, bringing us closer to His love and purpose for our lives.

Day 10 - Promise in the Process

IN LIFE, WE OFTEN FIND ourselves frustrated by struggles, delays, and setbacks that make it hard to understand why we face such challenges. It's in these moments that hope can feel distant, and we might wonder if our efforts and prayers are making any difference. But the Bible teaches us that there is a promise in the process, that God is with us in every step, working through every challenge to bring about a greater purpose. The process of growth, faith, and endurance is not without purpose; it is designed by God to shape us, strengthen us, and prepare us for the future He has planned. Romans 8:28 reminds us, "And we know that all things work together for good to them that love God, to them who are the called according to his purpose." This powerful verse assures us that God is actively working in our lives, taking every experience—good and bad—and using it for our good. Even when we can't see how it will all come together, God promises that every part of the journey is valuable and that no struggle is wasted. This is why it matters to find hope in moments of frustration; because God's promise is present even in the waiting, even in the struggle, and even when we feel weary. He is weaving together a plan that is greater than we can see, and His promise is that, in His perfect timing, we will see the good He has prepared for us.

In James 1:2-4, we are encouraged to look at trials in a new way: "My brethren, count it all joy when ye fall into divers temptations; Knowing this, that the trying of your faith worketh patience. But let patience have her perfect work, that ye may be perfect and entire, wanting nothing." This passage reminds us that the process of facing trials and frustrations is one that builds patience within us. Patience is a crucial part of the Christian journey, a way of learning to trust in God's timing and to believe that He knows what is best for us. When we go through trials, God is building resilience in our hearts, teaching us to hold onto faith even when we don't understand the path we're on. Patience allows us to grow, to deepen our relationship with God, and to trust that He is guiding us through each step, refining us like gold in the fire. This process of patience is a reminder that God's work in our lives is ongoing, that He is not finished with us, and that each challenge is part of His plan to make us more complete in Him.

The process also teaches us reliance on God, drawing us closer to Him in our times of need. In 2 Corinthians 12:9, God's promise is clear: "My grace is sufficient for thee: for my strength is made perfect in weakness." When we face moments of frustration, when we feel weak and uncertain, God's promise is that His grace will be enough for us. This promise is not just for moments of victory, but especially for times when we feel worn down by life's challenges. God's strength becomes our strength, His grace lifts us up, and His presence gives us the courage to keep going. In our weakness, God is at work, proving His power and showing us that He is our refuge and support. The process of depending on God teaches us humility and trust, helping us to understand that we don't have to face our struggles alone. God is with us, guiding us, comforting us, and giving us what we need to persevere. This reliance on God is part of the promise, a reminder that even in our hardest moments, He is our strength.

Another promise in the process is that of growth and transformation. In 2 Corinthians 3:18, we read, "But we all, with open face beholding as in a glass the glory of the Lord, are changed into the same image from glory to glory, even as by the Spirit of the Lord." God's work in us is continuous, transforming us step by step to become more like Christ. Each moment of frustration, every struggle and hardship, is an opportunity for growth. God is molding our character, shaping us into His image, teaching us to be compassionate, resilient, and faithful. The process is not easy, but it is purposeful, and God's promise is that each trial will bring us closer to Him, refining our hearts and minds to reflect His love. This transformation is a testament to God's faithfulness, showing us that He is working in us to bring out the best, even in difficult times.

The Bible also promises us that there is joy waiting at the end of the process. In Psalm 30:5, we are reminded, "Weeping may endure for a night, but joy cometh in the morning." This verse reassures us that our pain, frustration, and sorrow are not forever; God promises us joy, a joy that comes after the storm, a peace that follows the struggle. The process of waiting, of enduring hardship, teaches us to value joy even more deeply when it comes. God does not leave us in our sorrow; His promise is to bring us through it, to wipe away our tears, and to fill our hearts with joy that can only come from Him. This joy is part of the promise in the process, a reminder that our struggles are temporary, but God's love and joy are everlasting. Each moment of frustration brings us one step closer to the joy that God has promised, a joy that will replace our sorrows and renew our hope.

Furthermore, staying committed to the process allows us to see God's faithfulness unfold. In Lamentations 3:22-23, we are reminded of God's constant love: "It is of the Lord's mercies that we are not consumed, because his compassions fail not. They are new every morning: great is thy faithfulness." Each day of the process, God's mercies are new; He gives us what we need to make it through, filling our lives with His compassion and grace. His faithfulness is a foundation we can stand on, especially when we feel frustrated or weary. As we go through the process, we see God's faithfulness in the ways He provides, protects, and comforts us. This faithfulness is part of His promise, a reminder that He is always with us, helping us through each struggle and guiding us toward His purpose. Knowing that God's faithfulness is unchanging gives us the strength to stay in the process, to keep going, and to hold onto hope, even when it feels hard.

Ultimately, the promise in the process is one of hope. In Jeremiah 29:11, God speaks of His plans for us, saying, "For I know the thoughts that I think toward you, saith the Lord, thoughts of peace, and not of evil, to give you an expected end." This verse tells us that God's plans are for our good, for our peace, and for our future. Even when the process feels difficult, God's promise is that He is leading us to a place of hope, that He is bringing us closer to the future He has prepared. The process may involve trials, delays, and moments of frustration, but it is all leading to a purpose that God has designed. His plans are greater than our own, and His promise is that He will complete the work He has started in us. This hope gives us the strength to stay in the process, to trust that God is guiding us, and to believe that He will fulfill His promises in His perfect timing.

In moments of frustration, it matters to find hope in the process because God is with us, working in us and through us, shaping us according to His purpose. Each trial, each delay, and each challenge is part of the journey, a journey that leads us closer to God's promises. God's promise is woven into every part of the process, assuring us that our efforts are not in vain and that He is bringing us through to a place of peace, joy, and fulfillment. When we hold onto this hope, we find the strength to persevere, to trust, and to keep moving forward, knowing that God's promise is faithful and that He will never leave us. The process may be hard, but the promise is real, a promise of transformation, growth, and a future filled with God's goodness.

Day 11 - Prayers for Endurance and Strength

In life, we all face times of frustration and difficulty, moments that test our patience and strength and leave us feeling worn down and defeated. It is in these times that our prayers for endurance and strength become vital, carrying us through even when we feel we cannot go on. The Bible reminds us over and over again that in our weakest moments, God is our source of strength, and He hears our prayers, giving us the endurance we need to face every challenge. In Isaiah 40:31, we are told, "But they that wait upon the Lord shall renew their strength; they shall mount up with wings as eagles; they shall run, and not be weary; and they shall walk, and not faint." This powerful verse reassures us that when we turn to God in prayer, He renews our strength, lifting us up and helping us to continue on the path He has set before us. We may feel tired and overwhelmed, but God's promise is that He will give us what we need to endure, no matter how hard the journey becomes. Prayers for endurance are about more than just asking for help; they are about drawing close to God, trusting in His strength, and relying on His presence to carry us through every difficulty.

One of the reasons why prayers for endurance and strength matter is because they remind us that we do not have to face our struggles alone. In Psalm 46:1, we read, "God is our refuge and strength, a very present help in trouble." This verse reminds us that God is always with us, ready to help us and give us strength when we feel weak. When we pray for endurance, we are turning to God as our refuge, seeking His comfort and support in times of trouble. Prayer connects us to God, allowing us to pour out our fears, frustrations, and worries, knowing that He cares deeply for us and is there to listen. God is not distant; He is a constant presence, a source of strength that never fails. In our moments of frustration, when we feel like giving up, prayer helps us to remember that we are held in God's hands, that He is our safe place, and that He will never leave us.

The Bible also encourages us to pray for strength because it is through God's strength that we can endure any trial. In Philippians 4:13, we are reminded, "I can do all things through Christ which strengtheneth me." This powerful truth tells us that with God's strength, we can face any challenge, overcome any obstacle, and keep going, even when hope feels thin. When we pray for strength, we are inviting God to work in us, to fill us with His power, and to help us do what we cannot do on our own. God's strength is greater than any difficulty we face, and when we rely on Him, we find that we are able to endure, to keep moving forward, and to hold onto hope even in the hardest moments. Prayers for strength matter because they are an act of faith, a way of saying, "God, I trust You to carry me through this." Each prayer draws us closer to Him, reminding us that He is greater than any frustration or hardship we may face.

Prayers for endurance and strength also help us to build patience. In James 1:2-4, we are told, "My brethren, count it all joy when ye fall into divers temptations; Knowing this, that the trying of your faith worketh patience. But let patience have her perfect work, that ye may be perfect and entire, wanting nothing." This verse shows us that our struggles are not meaningless; they are opportunities to grow in patience and endurance. When we pray for endurance, we are asking God to help us develop the patience we need to keep going, to wait on His timing, and to trust that He has a purpose for every trial. Patience is not easy, but it is a vital part of our faith, teaching us to rely on God and to believe that He is working even when we cannot see it. Prayers for endurance build patience within us, helping us to become stronger, more resilient, and more grounded in our faith.

In times of frustration, when we feel weary and discouraged, prayer also brings us peace. Philippians 4:6-7 tells us, "Be careful for nothing; but in every thing by prayer and supplication with thanksgiving let your requests be made known unto God. And the peace of God, which passeth all understanding, shall keep your hearts and minds through Christ Jesus." This passage reminds us that prayer is not just about asking for strength; it is also about finding peace in God's presence. When we bring our struggles to God, He fills us with a peace that goes beyond our understanding, a peace that calms our hearts and gives us the courage to keep going. Prayers for endurance and strength are about seeking God's peace, about trusting that He is in control, and about finding rest in His promises. This peace helps us to face each day with hope, to keep moving forward even when the path is hard, and to trust that God is working all things together for our good.

The Bible also shows us that praying for strength and endurance brings us closer to God, helping us to grow in our relationship with Him. In 2 Corinthians 12:9, God speaks to Paul, saying, "My grace is sufficient for thee: for my strength is made perfect in weakness." This verse reminds us that it is often in our weakest moments that we experience God's strength the most. When we pray for endurance, we are acknowledging our need for God, allowing Him to work in us and to show us His power. God's grace is enough to carry us through any trial, and when we turn to Him in prayer, we open ourselves to His strength, His love, and His presence. Prayers for endurance deepen our faith, teaching us to rely on God more fully and to trust that He is with us, giving us everything we need to face life's challenges.

In moments of frustration, when we feel like we cannot go on, prayer becomes a lifeline, connecting us to the God who sustains us. Hebrews 4:16 encourages us, "Let us therefore come boldly unto the throne of grace, that we may obtain mercy, and find grace to help in time of need." This verse invites us to come to God with confidence, to bring our needs to Him and to seek His help in times of trouble. Prayers for endurance are a way of coming to God boldly, trusting that He is ready to help us, to give us the strength we need, and to show us His mercy. God's grace is always available to us, and when we pray, we receive His help, His comfort, and His guidance. Prayers for strength remind us that we are not alone in our struggles; God is with us, providing us with everything we need to endure.

Ultimately, prayers for endurance and strength matter because they are a way of holding onto hope. In Romans 15:13, we read, "Now the God of hope fill you with all joy and peace in believing, that ye may abound in hope, through the power of the Holy Ghost." This verse reminds us that God is the source of all hope, and that through prayer, we can find the joy and peace we need to continue. When we pray for endurance, we are asking God to fill us with His hope, to renew our spirits, and to help us see beyond our present struggles. God's hope gives us the strength to persevere, to believe that better days are ahead, and to trust that He is leading us through every trial. Each prayer is a reminder that God is faithful, that He will never leave us, and that He will give us the strength to endure, no matter how hard the journey may be.

In every moment of frustration, prayer connects us to God's power, His peace, and His presence, giving us the endurance we need to keep going.

Through prayer, we find strength to face each day, hope to carry us through, and peace to calm our hearts. Prayers for endurance and strength are about trusting that God is with us, that He hears our cries, and that He will give us what we need to overcome. These prayers remind us that we are not alone, that God's grace is sufficient, and that His strength is made perfect in our weakness. In every prayer, we find the courage to keep moving forward, to hold onto hope, and to believe that God is working all things together for our good. Prayer is our pathway to endurance, our source of strength, and our lifeline to the God who loves us and will never let us go.

Day 12 - Perceiving Hidden Progress

IN LIFE, IT'S EASY to get discouraged when we feel stuck, when our efforts seem to be going nowhere, and when frustration takes over because we don't see the results we hope for. But from a Biblical perspective, there is a powerful truth that reminds us why it matters to keep going, even when we can't see the full picture: God is always at work, even when progress is hidden from us. The Bible encourages us to perceive the hidden progress that God is making in our lives, to trust that He is working in ways we can't always see, and to hold on to hope even in moments of frustration. In Philippians 1:6, we are assured, "Being confident of this very thing, that he which hath begun a good work in you will perform it until the day of Jesus Christ." This verse reminds us that God is faithful, and if He has started a work in us, He will carry it through to completion. It may not always be visible or immediate, but God's hand is always guiding us, shaping us, and moving us toward His purpose. Hidden progress is not a sign of failure; rather, it is a sign that God's timing is at work, and He is developing something in us that is deeper and stronger than we may realize. When we face moments of frustration, we are invited to trust in this unseen progress, to believe that God is cultivating growth beneath the surface, even when it's hard to see it with our own eyes.

One of the reasons hidden progress matters is because it teaches us patience. In James 1:2-4, we are told, "My brethren, count it all joy when ye fall into divers temptations; Knowing this, that the trying of your faith worketh patience. But let patience have her perfect work, that ye may be perfect and entire, wanting nothing." This passage reminds us that trials and frustrations are opportunities for our faith to grow stronger, for our patience to deepen, and for our hearts to be refined. Hidden progress requires us to lean on God's timing rather than our own, to trust that He knows what is best and that He is working for our good. Each time we face frustration and choose to persevere, we are allowing God to build patience within us, preparing us for the future He has planned. Patience is not just about waiting; it's about trusting that God is moving, even when we can't see the steps He is taking. Hidden progress is God's way of teaching us to rely on Him, to find peace in His promises, and to know that His work in us is ongoing, even in the quiet seasons.

The Bible also shows us that hidden progress often happens when we are being molded and refined for something greater. In Isaiah 64:8, we read, "But now, O Lord, thou art our father; we are the clay, and thou our potter; and we all are the work of thy hand." Just as a potter shapes clay, God is shaping us, and sometimes this shaping happens in ways that are not immediately visible. The hidden progress in our lives is like the potter's hands, gently molding and refining us, smoothing out our rough edges, and creating something beautiful. This process can be uncomfortable and slow, but it is necessary for us to become who God created us to be. The frustration we feel during hidden progress is part of God's design, a way for us to let go of our own control and allow Him to do His work. When we trust God as the potter of our lives, we begin to see that every delay, every setback, and every hidden step is part of a bigger picture, one that is full of purpose and promise.

In moments of frustration, it's easy to feel like we're making no difference, but God calls us to walk by faith and not by sight. 2 Corinthians 5:7 reminds us, "For we walk by faith, not by sight." This verse challenges us to trust that God's work is not always visible but is always valuable. Hidden progress teaches us to lean on faith, to believe that God is working in the unseen, and to trust that He is moving us forward even when we feel like we are standing still. Walking by faith means believing that God's promises are true, that He is making a way for us, and that each step we take in obedience is bringing us closer to His purpose. Faith allows us to perceive hidden progress, to understand that what is unseen is often more important than what we can see, and to find hope in the quiet, unseen work of God in our lives.

Another reason why hidden progress matters is that it builds resilience. Romans 5:3-4 tells us, "And not only so, but we glory in tribulations also: knowing that tribulation worketh patience; And patience, experience; and experience, hope." This passage teaches us that hidden progress, especially in times of trial, is building resilience within us, a strength that can only be developed through perseverance. When we face frustration and keep moving forward, even when the results are hidden, we are growing in endurance, gaining experience, and deepening our hope. Each time we choose to trust God in the hidden moments, we are becoming more resilient, more able to withstand life's challenges, and more confident in God's faithfulness. Hidden progress reminds us that our struggles are not wasted; they are shaping us into people of endurance, preparing us for the blessings and responsibilities that God has in store.

The Bible also reassures us that hidden progress is often the foundation for future blessings. Galatians 6:9 encourages us, "And let us not be weary in well doing: for in due season we shall reap, if we faint not." This verse is a reminder that the seeds we plant, even when progress is hidden, will one day bear fruit. God sees our efforts, our prayers, and our faithfulness, even when we feel like nothing is changing. Each small act of obedience, each prayer lifted, and each step of faith is like a seed planted in the soil, waiting for the right time to grow. The hidden progress we experience is part of the planting season, a time of preparation that leads to a harvest we may not yet see. God's timing is perfect, and when we remain faithful, He promises that our efforts will be rewarded. Hidden progress is not a delay in God's plan; it is part of His perfect timing, a season of growth that will lead to blessings we cannot yet imagine.

In moments of hidden progress, prayer becomes our lifeline, a way to connect with God and to find encouragement in His presence. Philippians 4:6-7 reminds us, "Be careful for nothing; but in every thing by prayer and supplication with thanksgiving let your requests be made known unto God. And the peace of God, which passeth all understanding, shall keep your hearts and minds through Christ Jesus." When we feel frustrated by hidden progress, prayer gives us peace, helping us to release our worries and to trust in God's plan. Through prayer, we find comfort, strength, and a renewed sense of hope, knowing that God hears us and is working on our behalf. Prayer helps us to perceive the hidden progress in our lives, to remember that God is with us, and to find peace in the journey, even when we can't see the final destination.

Hidden progress also reminds us to focus on God's eternal promises rather than on temporary results. In 2 Corinthians 4:17-18, we are reminded, "For our light affliction, which is but for a moment, worketh for us a far more exceeding and eternal weight of glory; While we look not at the things which are seen, but at the things which are not seen: for the things which are seen are temporal; but the things which are not seen are eternal." This passage encourages us to look beyond our immediate frustrations and to focus on the eternal work God is doing in our lives. Hidden progress is often part of God's greater plan, a plan that reaches beyond our current struggles and leads us to a future filled with His glory. When we focus on God's eternal promises, we find hope, knowing that our present difficulties are only part of a larger picture, a picture that God is painting with purpose and love.

In every season of hidden progress, God is with us, guiding us, shaping us, and preparing us for the future He has planned. Hidden progress is not a sign of failure or delay; it is a reminder that God's ways are higher than our own and that He is at work even when we cannot see it. Each moment of frustration, each setback, and each unseen step is part of God's process, a process that leads us closer to Him and to the purpose He has for our lives. When we learn to perceive hidden progress, we begin to see our lives from God's perspective, to trust in His timing, and to find hope in His faithfulness. Hidden progress is a gift, a way for us to grow in faith, to build resilience, and to become the people God created us to be. Even in the quiet, unseen moments, God is at work, and His promise is that one day we will see the harvest of all He has planted in our hearts.

Day 13 - Preparation Through Life's Trials

Life is full of trials and challenges that often leave us feeling frustrated, discouraged, and worn down, making us wonder why we must endure so much difficulty. But from a Biblical perspective, every trial has a purpose, and each challenge we face is part of God's process of preparing us for the future He has planned. When we understand that our struggles are not random but are a way God shapes us, we can find hope even in the hardest times. The Bible teaches us that trials are like a refining fire, a way of removing what is unnecessary and making us stronger, more faithful, and closer to the people God created us to be. In James 1:2-4, we are encouraged to see our struggles with a new perspective: "My brethren, count it all joy when ye fall into divers temptations; Knowing this, that the trying of your faith worketh patience. But let patience have her perfect work, that ye may be perfect and entire, wanting nothing." This verse reminds us that our trials work within us, building patience and endurance, helping us grow stronger and more resilient. It's hard to see the purpose when we are in the middle of hardship, but God promises that these moments are not wasted; they are part of His plan to make us "perfect and entire," ready for the future blessings and responsibilities He has prepared for us. Preparation through life's trials is about more than just getting through hard times; it's about becoming the person God intended, someone who reflects His love, strength, and wisdom in every season.

One of the reasons why trials matter is because they build patience, a quality that is essential for walking in faith. Patience is not something we are born with; it is developed through waiting, trusting, and enduring. In Romans 5:3-4, we are told, "And not only so, but we glory in tribulations also: knowing that tribulation worketh patience; And patience, experience; and experience, hope." Trials teach us to wait on God's timing, to trust that He is in control, and to know that He is working even when we cannot see it. Each moment of frustration is an opportunity to lean into God's strength and to learn to rely on His wisdom rather than our own understanding. Patience is like a muscle that grows stronger each time we use it, and trials are the workout that builds our spiritual endurance. When we allow patience to grow within us, we are better prepared to face future challenges, knowing that God is faithful and that He will see us through every storm.

Trials also draw us closer to God, deepening our relationship with Him and teaching us to rely on His presence in every moment. In Psalm 34:18, we are reminded, "The Lord is nigh unto them that are of a broken heart; and saveth such as be of a contrite spirit." God draws near to us in our hardest moments, offering us comfort, strength, and peace. Our trials remind us of our need for Him, helping us to see that we cannot handle everything on our own. When life feels overwhelming, our struggles lead us to the feet of God, where we find the courage to keep going and the assurance that we are not alone. Through our trials, we learn to trust in God's promises, to seek His guidance, and to find peace in His presence. Each trial brings us one step closer to God, building a relationship rooted in faith, love, and trust.

Preparation through life's trials is also about building our character, shaping us to reflect God's goodness, patience, and compassion. In Romans 8:28-29, we are assured, "And we know that all things work together for good to them that love God, to them who are the called according to his purpose. For whom he did foreknow, he also did predestinate to be conformed to the image of his Son." This verse reminds us that our trials are part of God's plan to make us more like Christ. Through our struggles, we learn humility, empathy, and compassion. We become more aware of the pain of others, more willing to lend a helping hand, and more understanding of the struggles that others face. Our trials teach us to be kind, to forgive, and to show mercy, qualities that are at the heart of Christ's example. Each challenge is a step toward becoming more like Jesus, a journey that deepens our faith and strengthens our commitment to living out God's love in the world.

The Bible also shows us that trials prepare us to fulfill God's purpose for our lives. In Jeremiah 29:11, God assures us, "For I know the thoughts that I think toward you, saith the Lord, thoughts of peace, and not of evil, to give you an expected end." God has a plan for each of us, a future filled with hope and purpose. Our trials are part of the preparation for this plan, equipping us with the skills, experiences, and faith we need to walk in the calling God has given us. Each trial is like a lesson, teaching us something that will help us in the future, whether it's resilience, empathy, patience, or faith. God uses our struggles to prepare us, to make us ready for the blessings and responsibilities that lie ahead.

When we see our trials as preparation, we can find hope, knowing that God is working in every moment, shaping us for a future filled with His promise.

In moments of frustration, when we feel worn down by life's trials, prayer becomes our lifeline, a way to connect with God and to find strength in His presence. Philippians 4:6-7 encourages us, "Be careful for nothing; but in every thing by prayer and supplication with thanksgiving let your requests be made known unto God. And the peace of God, which passeth all understanding, shall keep your hearts and minds through Christ Jesus." Prayer helps us to release our worries, to lay down our burdens, and to find peace in God's love. When we bring our struggles to God in prayer, we are reminded that we are not alone, that He is with us, and that He is guiding us through every challenge. Prayer connects us to God's strength, helping us to endure, to find hope, and to remember that He is working even when we cannot see it. Through prayer, we find the courage to face each day, to keep moving forward, and to trust that God is using our trials to prepare us for something greater.

Preparation through life's trials also teaches us to focus on God's eternal promises rather than on our temporary struggles. In 2 Corinthians 4:17-18, we are reminded, "For our light affliction, which is but for a moment, worketh for us a far more exceeding and eternal weight of glory; While we look not at the things which are seen, but at the things which are not seen: for the things which are seen are temporal; but the things which are not seen are eternal." This passage encourages us to look beyond our present difficulties and to focus on the eternal work that God is doing in our lives. Our trials may be painful, but they are also temporary, and they are leading us to a future filled with God's glory. When we focus on God's promises, we find hope, knowing that our struggles are part of a larger plan, a plan that reaches beyond our current challenges and leads us to an eternal home with God. Each trial brings us one step closer to this future, a future filled with peace, joy, and the presence of God.

In every season of life, God uses our trials to prepare us, to build our faith, and to draw us closer to Him. Preparation through life's trials is not about enduring hardship for no reason; it is about growing, learning, and becoming more like Christ. Each moment of frustration, each setback, and each challenge is part of God's process, a process that leads us closer to His purpose and His promises. When we see our trials as preparation, we begin to understand that God is with us, working in every moment, and that He is using our struggles to make us stronger, wiser, and more faithful. Preparation through life's trials matters because it teaches us to trust God, to rely on His strength, and to believe that He is guiding us to a future filled with hope, love, and purpose.

Day 14 - Presence Over Perfection

In life, many of us strive for perfection, wanting everything to be just right—our actions, our decisions, even our relationships. We often set such high standards for ourselves, hoping to avoid mistakes or to gain approval, thinking that by being perfect, we will finally find peace and acceptance. But when perfection becomes our goal, frustration quickly follows. We end up feeling discouraged, disappointed, and weary because no matter how hard we try, perfection remains out of reach. From a Biblical perspective, however, God reminds us that what truly matters is not perfection, but His presence with us in every moment of life. God does not call us to be flawless; instead, He calls us to be faithful, to walk with Him, and to rely on His grace rather than our own abilities. In 2 Corinthians 12:9, we read, "And he said unto me, My grace is sufficient for thee: for my strength is made perfect in weakness." This verse reminds us that God's strength shines brightest in our weaknesses, and His grace fills the gaps where we fall short. It is in these moments of imperfection and struggle that God's presence becomes our greatest comfort, showing us that we do not have to be perfect to be loved, accepted, and used by Him. God's desire is not for us to achieve perfection, but to be present with Him, to seek His guidance, and to trust in His strength.

The Bible teaches us that God values our relationship with Him far more than any effort to achieve perfection. In Micah 6:8, we find a simple yet powerful reminder: "He hath shewed thee, O man, what is good; and what doth the Lord require of thee, but to do justly, and to love mercy, and to walk humbly with thy God?" This verse reminds us that what God desires is not flawless performance but a humble heart that seeks His presence. He calls us to walk with Him, to be near Him, and to trust Him with our lives. Walking with God means recognizing that we don't have to have it all together; we simply need to keep moving forward with faith, knowing that His grace is enough. Each time we choose presence over perfection, we are allowing God to work in us and through us, showing the world His love, mercy, and compassion. It is not our perfection that reveals God's greatness, but our willingness to lean on Him in our weakness. In every struggle, every mistake, and every moment of frustration, God is with us, reminding us that His love is not based on our achievements but on His grace.

Choosing presence over perfection also frees us from the weight of unrealistic expectations, allowing us to experience God's peace and joy even when life is far from perfect. Philippians 4:6-7 tells us, "Be careful for nothing; but in every thing by prayer and supplication with thanksgiving let your requests be made known unto God. And the peace of God, which passeth all understanding, shall keep your hearts and minds through Christ Jesus." This passage encourages us to bring our worries and frustrations to God, trusting that His presence will bring us peace. When we focus on being present with God rather than trying to perfect every detail, we find a sense of calm that the world cannot offer. God's peace is not dependent on everything being just right; it is a gift that comes from resting in His presence, knowing that He is in control. By letting go of perfection, we open our hearts to the peace that only God can give, a peace that carries us through every challenge and helps us to find joy even in the midst of life's imperfections.

The Bible also shows us that God's presence transforms our perspective, helping us to see our lives and our struggles through His eyes. In Psalm 46:10, we are reminded, "Be still, and know that I am God." This verse encourages us to pause, to be present with God, and to remember that He is greater than any problem we face. When we focus on God's presence, our worries and frustrations begin to fade, and we are reminded that He is with us, guiding us and carrying us through every difficulty. Being still in God's presence allows us to let go of our need for control, to trust that He is working in ways we cannot see, and to find peace in knowing that He holds our lives in His hands. God's presence gives us a sense of purpose and direction, showing us that we don't have to have it all figured out; we simply need to trust Him one step at a time.

Another reason why presence matters more than perfection is because it helps us to experience God's grace in a personal and powerful way. In Hebrews 4:16, we are invited, "Let us therefore come boldly unto the throne of grace, that we may obtain mercy, and find grace to help in time of need." This invitation reminds us that we can approach God freely, without fear or shame, knowing that He welcomes us just as we are. God's grace meets us in our imperfections, covering our weaknesses and filling us with His strength. When we focus on being present with God, we begin to understand that His grace is not just a concept but a daily gift that empowers us to live in freedom. We are not defined by our failures or shortcomings; we are defined by God's love and His grace that sustains us. In His presence, we find the courage to let go of perfectionism, to accept ourselves as we are, and to trust that God's grace is more than enough.

Presence over perfection also teaches us to love others with compassion and understanding, recognizing that we are all in need of God's grace. In Ephesians 4:2, we are encouraged, "With all lowliness and meekness, with longsuffering, forbearing one another in love." This verse reminds us that true love is not about expecting perfection from ourselves or others but about showing patience, kindness, and forgiveness. When we focus on presence, we become more aware of God's love for us, and this awareness helps us to extend that same love to others. We learn to accept people as they are, to offer grace instead of judgment, and to be a source of encouragement rather than criticism. Choosing presence over perfection helps us to build stronger, more compassionate relationships, rooted in God's love and grace. It reminds us that God's love is not based on our performance but on His unconditional acceptance, and this love flows through us to those around us.

Finally, choosing presence over perfection brings us closer to God's purpose for our lives. In Jeremiah 29:11, God declares, "For I know the thoughts that I think toward you, saith the Lord, thoughts of peace, and not of evil, to give you an expected end." God's plans for us are filled with hope and purpose, and He is more concerned with our hearts than with our accomplishments. When we focus on being present with God, we are more attuned to His guidance, more aware of His voice, and more open to the path He has prepared for us. God does not need us to be perfect to fulfill His plans; He simply asks us to be willing, to trust Him, and to walk with Him. In His presence, we find clarity, direction, and the assurance that He is leading us toward a future filled with His promises. By letting go of perfection, we make room for God's purpose to unfold in our lives, trusting that His plans are greater than anything we could achieve on our own.

In every moment of life, God calls us to choose His presence over perfection, to seek Him above all else, and to rest in the knowledge that we are loved, accepted, and valued just as we are. His grace is sufficient, His love is unchanging, and His presence is our greatest source of strength. When we focus on being present with God, we find freedom from the pressure to be perfect, peace in the midst of life's challenges, and hope that carries us through every frustration. God's presence is a constant reminder that we are not alone, that we are held by His love, and that His grace is enough for every moment. Choosing presence over perfection helps us to live in peace, to love with compassion, and to walk in faith, knowing that God is with us, guiding us every step of the way.

Day 15 - Possibility in Unexpected Places

In life, we all face moments of frustration when it feels like our efforts are going nowhere, when doors seem to close, and we wonder if there's any point in holding onto hope. These times can be discouraging, making us feel stuck or even abandoned. But the Bible teaches us that God often brings possibility in unexpected places, working through situations we didn't plan for or understand, using the very challenges and obstacles that seem impossible to bring about blessings we could have never imagined. This truth gives us hope, reminding us that with God, nothing is ever truly hopeless or wasted. In Romans 8:28, we find reassurance: "And we know that all things work together for good to them that love God, to them who are the called according to his purpose." This verse tells us that God is always at work, even when we can't see it, weaving every situation—good and bad—into a purpose that serves His greater plan for our lives. When we feel frustrated or defeated, God's promise assures us that possibility is still alive, even in the hardest of circumstances. Our struggles and setbacks are not the end of the story; rather, they are part of the journey that God uses to bring us closer to the blessings He has prepared. Possibility in unexpected places matters because it teaches us to trust in God's timing, to believe that He is opening doors we cannot see, and to hold onto hope, knowing that He can turn even our disappointments into something beautiful.

One of the most powerful lessons about possibility in unexpected places is the reminder that God's ways are often different from ours. In Isaiah 55:8-9, God declares, "For my thoughts are not your thoughts, neither are your ways my ways, saith the Lord. For as the heavens are higher than the earth, so are my ways higher than your ways, and my thoughts than your thoughts." This verse encourages us to trust that God's perspective is far greater than ours, that He sees the bigger picture when we can only see a small part. When we face unexpected situations, we can trust that God is working in ways that are beyond our understanding. He sees possibilities where we see problems, and He knows how to bring blessings out of burdens. Instead of giving up in frustration, we are invited to let go of our limited perspective and to trust that God is opening doors, even in places that seem closed. Each time we encounter an obstacle, we have a choice to either feel defeated or to trust that God is using it for a purpose, to believe that He can bring something good from it, even if we can't see how.

The Bible also shows us that God uses unexpected places and situations to strengthen our faith and teach us to rely on Him. In 2 Corinthians 12:9, Paul shares a powerful message he received from God: "And he said unto me, My grace is sufficient for thee: for my strength is made perfect in weakness." This verse reminds us that God's power is often most visible when we feel the weakest. When we reach the end of our own strength, God's strength becomes our source, showing us that He is able to carry us through situations that seem impossible. Possibility in unexpected places is not about our own ability but about God's power working in and through us. When we face challenges that feel too big, we are reminded to lean on God, to pray, and to trust that His grace is enough. In our weakness, He becomes our strength, turning obstacles into opportunities and using the unexpected moments of life to draw us closer to Him. When we look back, we often realize that it was in these hardest times that we grew the most, learned the most, and saw God's presence in ways we hadn't before.

Possibility in unexpected places also teaches us to keep our eyes open for God's blessings, even when they come in ways we didn't expect. In James 1:17, we are reminded, "Every good gift and every perfect gift is from above, and cometh down from the Father of lights, with whom is no variableness, neither shadow of turning." This verse assures us that God is the giver of all good things, even when they come in packages we didn't plan for. Sometimes, the blessings God has for us come disguised as challenges or changes in plans. An opportunity we never considered may open up a new path, a delay may bring us to something better, or a struggle may teach us something invaluable that prepares us for the future. When we remain open to the possibility that God is working in every situation, we begin to see His blessings even in the midst of frustration. Our faith grows as we recognize that God is the source of every good thing in our lives, guiding us, protecting us, and providing for us in ways we may not have expected.

The Bible also encourages us to believe that God can bring something beautiful out of what seems broken. In Joel 2:25, God promises, "And I will restore to you the years that the locust hath eaten." This powerful promise reminds us that God can take even the most painful, lost, or wasted moments and bring restoration. He has the power to redeem what seems broken, to heal what seems beyond repair, and to bring hope where there seemed to be none. When we feel like we've lost time, opportunities, or hope, God promises that He can restore what was taken, making something new out of what seemed lost. This is the possibility of unexpected places—the hope that God is not finished, that He can bring us to a place of healing, joy, and purpose, even from the broken pieces of our lives. God's promise of restoration gives us hope, helping us to believe that nothing is too far gone for Him to redeem.

Possibility in unexpected places also calls us to step out in faith, to trust that God is leading us even when we don't know the way. In Proverbs 3:5-6, we are encouraged, "Trust in the Lord with all thine heart; and lean not unto thine own understanding. In all thy ways acknowledge him, and he shall direct thy paths." This verse reminds us that we don't have to understand everything to trust God. When we acknowledge Him, He promises to guide us, even through unexpected twists and turns. God often brings us to places we never planned to be, but when we trust Him, we find that He is leading us to something better, something we couldn't have found on our own. Each step of faith we take, especially in uncertain times, is a step closer to the possibilities God has for us. We learn to let go of our own plans and to embrace the journey, trusting that God's path is leading us exactly where we need to be.

In every moment of frustration, the possibility in unexpected places gives us hope, reminding us that God's plans are always greater than our own. When we feel stuck or discouraged, we can find encouragement in God's promise that He is working, that He is with us, and that He will bring us through. The Bible shows us over and over that God uses the unexpected to bring about His will, transforming ordinary moments into extraordinary blessings. As we learn to trust Him, to see His hand in every situation, and to believe that He is working all things for our good, we find the strength to keep going, knowing that God's possibilities are endless. In unexpected places, God does His greatest work, turning obstacles into stepping stones, turning setbacks into setups for His glory, and turning our frustration into a renewed hope.

Day 16 - Proof of Purpose Through Perseverance

In life, we often find ourselves in situations that test our limits, where frustration builds and hope seems like a distant dream. These are the moments that push us to our edge, making us wonder if there's any point to the struggle. But from a Biblical perspective, these very moments of hardship and frustration are the places where God reveals His purpose for our lives, showing us that our perseverance is not in vain. In James 1:12, we read, "Blessed is the man that endureth temptation: for when he is tried, he shall receive the crown of life, which the Lord hath promised to them that love him." This verse reminds us that there is a blessing in perseverance, a purpose in pushing through, even when the journey is difficult. Our efforts are not wasted; they are part of a larger plan that God is unfolding. Proof of purpose comes through perseverance, for it is in these hard-fought battles that God shapes us, teaches us, and prepares us for the blessings He has in store. The Bible shows us over and over again that endurance is not just about surviving; it's about thriving in faith, about holding on to hope when everything else says to give up, and about finding strength in God's promises. Perseverance matters because it transforms us, builds our character, and brings us closer to the life God has called us to live.

One of the most important lessons about proof of purpose through perseverance is that God often uses our challenges to prepare us for something greater. In Romans 5:3-4, we are reminded, "And not only so, but we glory in tribulations also: knowing that tribulation worketh patience; And patience, experience; and experience, hope." This verse shows us that the trials we face are not meaningless; they are part of a process that builds patience, strengthens our experience, and ultimately fills us with hope. Every time we persevere through a difficult season, we are learning to trust God more deeply, to lean on His strength, and to grow in faith. Patience is a quality that cannot be learned in comfort; it is built in the struggles and the waiting. Through perseverance, we become more resilient, more grounded, and more prepared for the blessings God has for us. Our struggles are not detours; they are stepping stones that lead us to the purpose God has prepared. Each moment of perseverance is proof that

God is working in us, refining our hearts, and equipping us for the future He has designed.

Perseverance also proves our faith, showing that we are committed to God's plan, even when it doesn't make sense. In Hebrews 11:1, we are told, "Now faith is the substance of things hoped for, the evidence of things not seen." Faith is about believing in God's promises, even when we cannot see the outcome. Perseverance is an act of faith, a way of saying, "God, I trust You, even when the way is unclear." Each time we choose to keep going, to hold onto hope, and to trust in God's plan, we are proving our faith. We are showing that we believe God is greater than our circumstances and that His promises are worth waiting for. Perseverance is proof that we are willing to walk by faith, to trust in the unseen, and to believe that God is working in ways we cannot yet understand. Our faith grows stronger with each step, and our relationship with God deepens as we learn to rely on Him in every season of life.

The Bible also shows us that perseverance builds our character, shaping us into the people God created us to be. In Romans 8:28-29, we read, "And we know that all things work together for good to them that love God, to them who are the called according to his purpose. For whom he did foreknow, he also did predestinate to be conformed to the image of his Son." This passage tells us that God's purpose is to make us more like Jesus, to shape us into His image. Perseverance through trials is one of the ways God does this. Each struggle, each moment of endurance, is a step toward becoming more compassionate, more patient, and more loving. Our character is refined in the fires of difficulty, teaching us humility, resilience, and faithfulness. As we persevere, we are being molded to reflect Christ's love, grace, and strength. Proof of purpose through perseverance is seen in the way our character grows, in the way we become more Christlike, and in the way we learn to love others with compassion and understanding.

Another reason why perseverance matters is because it leads us to the blessings that God has promised. In Galatians 6:9, we are encouraged, "And let us not be weary in well doing: for in due season we shall reap, if we faint not." This verse reminds us that perseverance brings a reward, that our efforts are not in vain. When we stay committed, when we keep pressing forward despite the hardships, we are moving closer to the blessings God has prepared. The harvest comes to those who do not give up, to those who believe that God's promises are true and that His timing is perfect. Perseverance teaches us to wait on God, to trust that He is working behind the scenes, and to believe that our season of blessing is coming. Proof of purpose is found in the harvest, in the moments when we see God's faithfulness come to life, and in the rewards that come from not giving up. Each time we persevere, we are sowing seeds of faith that will one day bear fruit, showing us that God's promises are worth the wait.

Perseverance also draws us closer to God, deepening our relationship with Him and teaching us to rely on His strength. In 2 Corinthians 12:9, God tells Paul, "My grace is sufficient for thee: for my strength is made perfect in weakness." This verse reminds us that God's strength becomes our own when we feel weak, that His grace is enough to carry us through every challenge. Perseverance teaches us to depend on God, to recognize that we cannot do everything on our own, and to find our strength in His presence. When we persevere, we are learning to trust God more fully, to rely on His guidance, and to find peace in knowing that He is with us every step of the way. Our relationship with God grows as we persevere, as we learn to seek Him in our struggles, and as we experience His love and faithfulness in the midst of our trials. Proof of purpose through perseverance is seen in the closeness we develop with God, in the way we learn to trust Him, and in the way His presence becomes our refuge.

Finally, perseverance teaches us to focus on God's eternal promises rather than on our temporary struggles. In 2 Corinthians 4:17-18, Paul writes, "For our light affliction, which is but for a moment, worketh for us a far more exceeding and eternal weight of glory; While we look not at the things which are seen, but at the things which are not seen: for the things which are seen are temporal; but the things which are not seen are eternal." This passage encourages us to look beyond our present difficulties and to focus on the eternal rewards that God has prepared. Perseverance reminds us that our struggles are temporary, but the blessings of eternity are forever. When we keep our eyes on God's promises, we find the strength to endure, knowing that our efforts are not in vain and that God has something greater in store. Proof of purpose through perseverance is seen in our ability to hold onto hope, to believe in God's promises, and to trust that He is leading us to a future filled with His glory.

In every moment of frustration, proof of purpose through perseverance reminds us that God is at work, shaping us, guiding us, and preparing us for the future He has planned. Each challenge, each step of endurance, is part of a process that leads us closer to God's purpose and His promises. Perseverance is not just about getting through hard times; it's about becoming stronger, growing in faith, and experiencing God's presence in deeper ways. Proof of purpose is found in the growth of our character, in the strengthening of our faith, and in the blessings that come from not giving up. When we choose to persevere, we are choosing to believe that God's plan is greater than our struggles, that His promises are worth the wait, and that His purpose will be fulfilled in His perfect timing.

Day 17 - Patterns of Growth in Adversity

IN LIFE, ADVERSITY can make us feel overwhelmed, discouraged, and frustrated. We often wonder why we have to face such difficult times, and we may even feel abandoned or lost in these dark moments. But the Bible teaches us that adversity is not only a part of life, but it's also a powerful tool that God uses to help us grow and become stronger. Through adversity, God shapes us, molds us, and builds our character. In James 1:2-4, we read, "My brethren, count it all joy when ye fall into divers temptations; Knowing this, that the trying of your faith worketh patience. But let patience have her perfect work, that ye may be perfect and entire, wanting nothing." This verse reminds us that the trials we face are not meaningless; they have a purpose. Each challenge and struggle works to develop patience within us, helping us become complete and strong in our faith. Adversity becomes a classroom where God teaches us patience, resilience, and trust in Him. When we face hardships, it's an opportunity for us to grow, to become more like Christ, and to deepen our relationship with God. Instead of giving in to frustration, we can choose to see these tough times as moments of growth, believing that God is with us, guiding us, and helping us through every step of the journey. Patterns of growth in adversity matter because they show us that God has a purpose for our struggles, and that each trial is a step toward becoming who He created us to be.

One of the most powerful ways that adversity helps us grow is by teaching us to rely on God. When life is easy, it's natural to rely on our own strength and abilities, but in difficult times, we realize that we can't do it all on our own. In Psalm 46:1, we are reminded, "God is our refuge and strength, a very present help in trouble." This verse tells us that God is there for us in every moment of need, ready to be our strength when we are weak. Adversity draws us closer to God, reminding us that we need His help, His guidance, and His presence in our lives. Each time we turn to Him in our struggles, we deepen our relationship with Him, learning to trust Him more fully. Relying on God in adversity is a lesson that stays with us, helping us to remember that He is our rock and our refuge, no matter what we face. Each challenge becomes a chance to lean on God and to discover His strength working within us.

Adversity also builds resilience, teaching us to endure and remain strong even when things get tough. In Romans 5:3-4, we read, "And not only so, but we glory in tribulations also: knowing that tribulation worketh patience; And patience, experience; and experience, hope." This verse shows us that adversity is part of a process that leads to greater strength and hope. Each trial teaches us patience, and that patience builds experience, helping us to trust God more deeply. As we go through adversity, we develop resilience, learning that we can withstand hardships and that God will see us through. This resilience is a powerful gift that keeps us steady and strong, helping us to hold onto hope even when life seems overwhelming. Adversity teaches us that we are stronger than we think, especially when we have God by our side. Each time we overcome a challenge, our faith grows, and we become better prepared for the next trial that may come our way.

The Bible also teaches us that adversity helps to refine our character, making us more compassionate, humble, and wise. In 1 Peter 1:6-7, we read, "Wherein ye greatly rejoice, though now for a season, if need be, ye are in heaviness through manifold temptations: That the trial of your faith, being much more precious than of gold that perisheth, though it be tried with fire, might be found unto praise and honour and glory at the appearing of Jesus Christ." Just as gold is refined by fire to remove impurities, adversity serves as a refining process for our hearts and minds. Hardships strip away our pride, teaching us humility and compassion for others who are also struggling. We learn to be more understanding, kind, and patient, knowing that everyone faces battles of their own. Adversity shapes us, helping us to grow in character and to become more like Christ, reflecting His love, grace, and strength in all that we do. Through each trial, God is refining us, helping us to become the people He created us to be, and preparing us to fulfill His purpose.

Another way adversity helps us grow is by strengthening our faith. In 2 Corinthians 12:9, God tells Paul, "My grace is sufficient for thee: for my strength is made perfect in weakness." This verse reminds us that God's grace and strength are most evident when we feel weak. When we face situations that we cannot handle on our own, we are reminded of our need for God's help. Adversity teaches us to depend on God's grace, to rely on His strength, and to trust that He is working, even when we can't see the outcome. Each time we experience His presence in our struggles, our faith grows stronger. We begin to see that God is faithful, that He never leaves us, and that His strength is more than enough to carry us through. Adversity becomes a training ground for our faith, teaching us to trust God's promises and to hold onto hope, knowing that He is always with us.

Adversity also reminds us of God's greater purpose for our lives, helping us to see that our struggles are part of a bigger picture. In Romans 8:28, we read, "And we know that all things work together for good to them that love God, to them who are the called according to his purpose." This verse assures us that God can use every experience, even the painful ones, for our good. Each time we go through adversity, we are moving closer to the purpose that God has planned for us. Our struggles are not meaningless; they are steps along the path that God has set for our lives. Adversity teaches us to trust in God's purpose, to believe that He is working behind the scenes, and to know that He can bring something beautiful out of even the hardest situations. When we see our struggles as part of God's plan, we find hope, knowing that He is guiding us and that He is using every experience to shape our future.

Finally, adversity gives us the strength to encourage others who may be going through similar struggles. In 2 Corinthians 1:3-4, Paul writes, "Blessed be God, even the Father of our Lord Jesus Christ, the Father of mercies, and the God of all comfort; Who comforteth us in all our tribulation, that we may be able to comfort them which are in any trouble, by the comfort wherewith we ourselves are comforted of God." This verse reminds us that the comfort we receive from God in our own struggles enables us to comfort others. Each time we face adversity, we gain wisdom, understanding, and empathy that allow us to support and encourage others who are going through hard times. Adversity makes us more compassionate and willing to reach out to those in need. We become vessels of God's love and comfort, sharing the hope and strength we've found in Him. Our own experiences of hardship become testimonies of God's faithfulness, helping others to see that they are not alone and that there is hope in every situation.

In every moment of adversity, God is with us, guiding us, strengthening us, and helping us grow. Patterns of growth in adversity reveal God's purpose, showing us that each trial is part of His plan to make us more like Christ. Each challenge becomes an opportunity to deepen our faith, to grow in character, and to draw closer to God. Adversity teaches us to rely on God, to find strength in His presence, and to trust in His promises. When we see our struggles as part of a larger picture, we find hope, knowing that God is working in every moment to bring about His will. Patterns of growth in adversity matter because they show us that God has a purpose for our lives, and that He is using every experience to prepare us for the future He has planned.

Day 18 - Pressing On When the Way is Hard

In life, there are seasons when the way feels incredibly hard, and every step forward seems to be met with resistance, frustration, or disappointment. It is in these difficult times that hope can feel distant, and it's tempting to consider giving up, wondering if the struggle is worth it. But the Bible teaches us that pressing on, even when the way is hard, is part of God's plan for building our strength, our character, and our faith. God does not promise us a life free from hardship, but He promises to be with us every step of the way, guiding us, strengthening us, and giving us the courage to keep moving forward. In Galatians 6:9, we are encouraged, "And let us not be weary in well doing: for in due season we shall reap, if we faint not." This powerful reminder shows us that our efforts are not in vain, that every step we take matters, and that God sees our perseverance. Pressing on, even when the way is hard, allows us to grow, to become more resilient, and to see God's faithfulness in ways we never could if we stopped at the first sign of difficulty. Every time we choose to press on, we are showing God that we trust Him, that we believe His promises are true, and that we are willing to keep moving forward because we know He is leading us.

One of the most important reasons to press on when the way is hard is because each step of endurance brings us closer to God's purpose for our lives. In Romans 5:3-4, we read, "And not only so, but we glory in tribulations also: knowing that tribulation worketh patience; And patience, experience; and experience, hope." This verse reminds us that every trial we face has a purpose. The challenges we endure work to develop patience within us, teaching us to rely on God's timing and to trust that He knows what is best for us. Patience is a quality that is only truly developed in difficult times, and it is this patience that allows us to grow stronger and more resilient in our faith. Each time we press on, we are building character, learning to trust God more deeply, and discovering a hope that goes beyond our circumstances. Our perseverance becomes a testament to our faith, a way of saying, "God, I trust You, even when the path is hard." This trust is what builds our faith, helping us to believe that God is with us and that He is working all things together for our good.

Pressing on also teaches us the power of relying on God's strength instead of our own. In 2 Corinthians 12:9, God tells Paul, "My grace is sufficient for thee: for my strength is made perfect in weakness." This verse reminds us that God's strength is most evident when we are weak. When we feel like we can't go on, when our own strength has run out, God's power becomes our source of strength. Pressing on allows us to experience God's grace in a personal and powerful way, showing us that we don't have to carry our burdens alone. God is with us, offering His strength, His comfort, and His guidance. Each time we take a step forward, even when it's hard, we are learning to lean on God more fully, trusting that He is carrying us and that His grace is enough. This reliance on God's strength is what helps us to press on, knowing that we are not alone and that we can do all things through Christ who strengthens us.

The Bible also encourages us to press on because there is a reward for those who endure. In James 1:12, we read, "Blessed is the man that endureth temptation: for when he is tried, he shall receive the crown of life, which the Lord hath promised to them that love him." This verse reminds us that God honors our perseverance, that He sees our struggles, and that there is a reward waiting for us when we choose to keep going. Pressing on is not just about getting through hard times; it's about showing God that we are faithful, that we are willing to endure, and that we believe His promises are true. Each moment of perseverance is a step toward the blessings that God has prepared for us, a reminder that our efforts are not in vain. When we press on, we are sowing seeds of faith that will one day bear fruit, showing us that God's promises are worth waiting for and that His rewards are worth the journey.

Another reason why pressing on matters is because it brings us closer to God. In Psalm 34:18, we are reminded, "The Lord is nigh unto them that are of a broken heart; and saveth such as be of a contrite spirit." This verse tells us that God draws near to us in our hardest moments, offering His comfort, His peace, and His presence. Pressing on through hard times brings us closer to God, teaching us to rely on Him, to seek His guidance, and to find strength in His presence. Each step we take is an opportunity to deepen our relationship with God, to experience His love and faithfulness, and to grow in our understanding of who He is. Pressing on helps us to see that God is with us, that He never leaves us, and that He is working in every situation for our good. Our relationship with God becomes stronger as we learn to trust Him in the valleys, knowing that He is our shepherd, guiding us through every dark and difficult place.

Pressing on also helps us to see the bigger picture, to understand that our struggles are part of a larger plan that God is unfolding. In 2 Corinthians 4:17-18, we are reminded, "For our light affliction, which is but for a moment, worketh for us a far more exceeding and eternal weight of glory; While we look not at the things which are seen, but at the things which are not seen: for the things which are seen are temporal; but the things which are not seen are eternal." This verse encourages us to look beyond our immediate struggles and to focus on the eternal rewards that God has prepared for us. Pressing on helps us to see that our current difficulties are only temporary, and that God has something greater in store. When we keep our eyes on the bigger picture, we find the strength to endure, knowing that our efforts are not wasted and that God's purpose is being fulfilled. Pressing on is about holding onto hope, believing that God is working behind the scenes, and trusting that He will bring us through to a future filled with His glory.

In every moment of frustration, pressing on is a choice to trust in God's plan, to believe in His promises, and to find hope in His presence. It is a decision to keep moving forward, even when the way is hard, knowing that God is with us, guiding us, and giving us the strength to endure. Each step we take brings us closer to His purpose, builds our character, and strengthens our faith. Pressing on when the way is hard is about more than just surviving; it's about thriving in faith, about holding onto hope, and about discovering that God's grace is sufficient for every challenge we face. When we press on, we are showing God that we believe in His love, that we trust in His promises, and that we are willing to follow Him wherever He leads. Pressing on matters because it leads us to the blessings God has prepared, it draws us closer to Him, and it reminds us that we are never alone. God is with us every step of the way, offering His strength, His peace, and His hope, helping us to press on toward the future He has planned.

Day 19 - Purifying Purpose in the Struggle

In life, we often go through struggles that test our patience, faith, and endurance, leaving us feeling frustrated and questioning why we have to face so many difficulties. From a Biblical perspective, these struggles are not without purpose; in fact, God uses them to purify our hearts, strengthen our spirits, and draw us closer to Him. Struggles are like a refining fire, removing the impurities and weaknesses that keep us from growing in faith and becoming the people God created us to be. In 1 Peter 1:6-7, we find powerful encouragement: "Wherein ye greatly rejoice, though now for a season, if need be, ye are in heaviness through manifold temptations: That the trial of your faith, being much more precious than of gold that perisheth, though it be tried with fire, might be found unto praise and honour and glory at the appearing of Jesus Christ." This verse reminds us that our trials serve a higher purpose, refining our faith and proving its worth. Just as gold is purified by fire to become more valuable, our faith is made stronger and purer through the struggles we endure. The purifying purpose in the struggle is a profound reminder that our hardships are not wasted, and they are not punishment; they are God's way of shaping us, teaching us, and preparing us for the blessings and responsibilities He has in store. Each struggle we face is an opportunity to trust God more deeply, to let go of what holds us back, and to find hope in His presence.

One of the most meaningful aspects of the purifying purpose in the struggle is that it draws us closer to God, helping us to rely on Him in ways we never would if life were always easy. In 2 Corinthians 12:9, God tells Paul, "My grace is sufficient for thee: for my strength is made perfect in weakness." This powerful truth shows us that God's strength becomes our strength, especially when we feel weak or discouraged. Struggles remind us of our need for God, showing us that we cannot handle everything on our own and that His grace is all we need to carry on. When we face difficult times, we learn to lean on God's promises, to seek His guidance, and to trust that He is with us in every moment. This reliance on God deepens our relationship with Him, teaching us to depend on His strength and to find comfort in His presence. The purifying purpose in the struggle reminds us that God is always near, that He is our refuge and strength, and that His grace is sufficient for whatever we face.

Struggles also help to build our character, teaching us patience, compassion, and humility. In Romans 5:3-4, we are reminded, "And not only so, but we glory in tribulations also: knowing that tribulation worketh patience; And patience, experience; and experience, hope." This passage shows us that struggles are part of a process that leads to growth. Each trial we face teaches us patience, helping us to endure and to trust in God's timing rather than our own. Patience is a quality that can only be developed through challenges; it is a strength that grows each time we choose to keep going, even when the way is hard. Struggles also teach us compassion, helping us to understand the pain of others and to reach out with kindness and empathy. Each hardship softens our hearts, showing us that everyone faces battles of their own and helping us to become more loving and understanding. Humility is another gift that comes from struggle, as we learn to let go of pride and to recognize that we need God's help in every part of our lives. Through the purifying purpose in the struggle, we become more like Christ, reflecting His love, patience, and humility in all that we do.

Another reason why struggles matter is that they prepare us for the purpose God has planned for us. In Jeremiah 29:11, God declares, "For I know the thoughts that I think toward you, saith the Lord, thoughts of peace, and not of evil, to give you an expected end." This verse reassures us that God has a purpose for each of us, a plan filled with hope and promise. The struggles we go through are part of the preparation for that purpose, equipping us with the strength, wisdom, and resilience we need to fulfill God's plan. Each hardship is like a lesson, teaching us skills, insights, and values that will help us in the future. Just as an athlete trains through hard workouts to become stronger, we are strengthened through our struggles, becoming more prepared for the work God has for us. The purifying purpose in the struggle shows us that each trial is part of a bigger picture, a picture that God is painting with purpose and love. When we trust that our struggles have meaning, we find hope, knowing that God is using each challenge to prepare us for something greater.

The Bible also reminds us that struggles help us to focus on what truly matters, to let go of temporary distractions, and to keep our eyes on God's eternal promises. In 2 Corinthians 4:17-18, we are encouraged, "For our light affliction, which is but for a moment, worketh for us a far more exceeding and eternal weight of glory; While we look not at the things which are seen, but at the things which are not seen: for the things which are seen are temporal; but the things which are not seen are eternal." This passage shows us that our struggles are temporary, but the rewards of perseverance are eternal. When we go through hardships, we are reminded to focus on God's promises, to value the things that last forever, and to keep our eyes on the hope of heaven. The purifying purpose in the struggle helps us to see beyond our present difficulties and to hold onto the hope that God is with us, guiding us toward an eternal future filled with His glory.

Through our struggles, we also become testimonies of God's faithfulness, able to encourage and support others who may be going through similar challenges. In 2 Corinthians 1:3-4, Paul writes, "Blessed be God, even the Father of our Lord Jesus Christ, the Father of mercies, and the God of all comfort; Who comforteth us in all our tribulation, that we may be able to comfort them which are in any trouble, by the comfort wherewith we ourselves are comforted of God." This verse shows us that the comfort we receive from God in our struggles enables us to share that comfort with others. Each trial we face becomes a story of God's faithfulness, a reminder that He is with us and that He never leaves us alone. The purifying purpose in the struggle not only strengthens our faith but also allows us to be a source of hope and encouragement to those around us. Our struggles become testimonies, showing others that God is real, that His love is powerful, and that His grace is enough for every need.

In every moment of struggle, God is with us, guiding us, refining us, and helping us grow. The purifying purpose in the struggle is a reminder that each hardship has meaning, that each trial is part of God's plan to make us stronger, wiser, and more faithful. Through our struggles, we learn to rely on God, to find hope in His promises, and to become more like Christ. Each challenge is an opportunity to draw closer to God, to trust in His grace, and to let go of what holds us back. When we see our struggles as part of God's process of growth and refinement, we find hope, knowing that He is working in every moment to bring about His purpose for our lives. The purifying purpose in the struggle matters because it teaches us to trust God, to rely on His strength, and to believe that He is guiding us toward a future filled with hope, love, and purpose.

Day 20 - Precious Lessons from Hard Times

In life, hard times come to everyone, bringing moments of frustration, disappointment, and sorrow. These times can make us feel like everything is against us, and we often wonder why we have to go through so much pain. But the Bible teaches us that even in the darkest valleys, God has a purpose, and He is teaching us precious lessons that will strengthen our faith, deepen our understanding, and draw us closer to Him. Hard times are not just painful experiences; they are opportunities for growth, windows through which we can see God's grace and love working in ways we might not have noticed before. In Romans 8:28, we are reminded, "And we know that all things work together for good to them that love God, to them who are the called according to his purpose." This verse assures us that no matter what we face, God is using every situation for our good. Even when it's hard to see or understand, God's hand is at work, guiding us, shaping us, and bringing us closer to the purpose He has for our lives. Precious lessons from hard times show us that our struggles are not wasted and that every tear, every hardship, and every frustration is a part of God's plan to refine us, teach us, and prepare us for what lies ahead.

One of the most valuable lessons we learn from hard times is the importance of trusting God. In Proverbs 3:5-6, we read, "Trust in the Lord with all thine heart; and lean not unto thine own understanding. In all thy ways acknowledge him, and he shall direct thy paths." This verse reminds us that our understanding is limited, but God's wisdom is infinite. During hard times, when we don't know why things are happening or how they will turn out, we learn to lean on God and trust His plan. Trusting God means letting go of our need to control everything and believing that He is working, even when we can't see it. Hard times teach us to walk by faith, to rely on God's promises, and to believe that He is guiding us in ways we may not understand until later. This lesson of trust is precious because it strengthens our relationship with God, showing us that He is faithful, that He will never leave us, and that His plans are always for our good.

Hard times also teach us the value of patience. In James 1:2-4, we are encouraged, "My brethren, count it all joy when ye fall into divers temptations; Knowing this, that the trying of your faith worketh patience. But let patience have her perfect work, that ye may be perfect and entire, wanting nothing." This passage shows us that patience is not just about waiting; it's about growing in strength, learning to endure, and trusting that God's timing is perfect. Patience helps us to stay steady, even when things are difficult, and to keep moving forward, even when we don't see immediate results. Hard times develop patience within us, showing us that good things often come through endurance. As we learn to be patient, we find peace in knowing that God's plan is unfolding, even if it's not happening as quickly as we'd like. This lesson of patience is precious because it teaches us to wait on God, to trust in His timing, and to believe that His ways are higher than our own.

Another lesson we learn from hard times is the importance of compassion. When we go through difficult moments, we begin to understand the struggles that others face, and our hearts become softer, more willing to reach out and help. In 2 Corinthians 1:3-4, Paul writes, "Blessed be God, even the Father of our Lord Jesus Christ, the Father of mercies, and the God of all comfort; Who comforteth us in all our tribulation, that we may be able to comfort them which are in any trouble, by the comfort wherewith we ourselves are comforted of God." This verse reminds us that the comfort we receive from God in our own struggles allows us to comfort others. Hard times teach us empathy, helping us to be more understanding, compassionate, and willing to support those who are hurting. This lesson of compassion is precious because it shows us how to love others with the same love God has shown us, creating connections that bring healing and hope.

Through hard times, we also learn the strength of resilience. In 2 Corinthians 4:8-9, we read, "We are troubled on every side, yet not distressed; we are perplexed, but not in despair; Persecuted, but not forsaken; cast down, but not destroyed." This passage reminds us that while hard times may knock us down, they do not have the power to destroy us when we have God by our side. Hard times build resilience within us, teaching us that we can face difficulties and come out stronger. Each time we get back up after a setback, our faith grows, and we become more confident in God's ability to carry us through. Resilience is the ability to keep going, to keep believing, and to keep hoping, even when life is challenging. This lesson of resilience is precious because it reminds us that we are never alone, that God is our strength, and that with Him, we can overcome any obstacle.

Hard times also remind us of the importance of humility. In moments of struggle, we realize our limitations, our weaknesses, and our need for God's help. In 2 Corinthians 12:9, God tells Paul, "My grace is sufficient for thee: for my strength is made perfect in weakness." This verse teaches us that our weaknesses are not something to be ashamed of; they are places where God's strength can shine. Hard times humble us, helping us to see that we cannot do everything on our own and that we need God's grace to sustain us. This lesson of humility is precious because it leads us to a place of surrender, where we can fully rely on God and allow His strength to work in us. Humility helps us to see ourselves more clearly and to understand that God's power is at work, even in our weakest moments.

Hard times also teach us gratitude. When we face challenges, we begin to appreciate the blessings we may have taken for granted. In 1 Thessalonians 5:18, we are encouraged, "In every thing give thanks: for this is the will of God in Christ Jesus concerning you." This verse reminds us that gratitude is not just for the good times; it's for every season of life. Hard times open our eyes to the small blessings around us, teaching us to be thankful for each day, each provision, and each moment of grace. Gratitude changes our perspective, helping us to see that even in difficulty, God's goodness is present. This lesson of gratitude is precious because it fills our hearts with joy, helps us to focus on the positive, and brings us closer to God, who is the giver of every good gift.

Finally, hard times teach us about hope. In Romans 15:13, we read, "Now the God of hope fill you with all joy and peace in believing, that ye may abound in hope, through the power of the Holy Ghost." This verse reminds us that God is the source of our hope, and that even in the darkest moments, He is with us, offering joy and peace. Hard times teach us to hold onto hope, to believe that God's promises are true, and to trust that He is working for our good. Hope is the anchor that keeps us steady, the light that guides us through the storm, and the assurance that God's plan is greater than our struggles. This lesson of hope is precious because it reminds us that with God, there is always a reason to keep going, always a future worth fighting for, and always a purpose in the pain.

In every season of hardship, God is teaching us precious lessons that shape our hearts, build our character, and draw us closer to Him. These lessons are gifts that strengthen our faith, deepen our trust, and help us to see life through His eyes. Hard times are not wasted moments; they are times of growth, transformation, and discovery. The lessons we learn through adversity become the foundation of our faith, the wisdom that guides us, and the strength that carries us forward. Precious lessons from hard times matter because they remind us that God is with us, that He is working in every situation, and that He is using each experience to make us stronger, wiser, and more like Christ. In the end, we emerge from hard times with a deeper understanding of God's love, a greater sense of purpose, and a heart that is filled with hope, knowing that we are never alone and that God's grace is enough for every moment of life.

Day 21 - Provision in Moments of Doubt

In life, there are times when doubt creeps in, and it feels like hope is slipping away. We all face moments of frustration when we wonder if we'll have enough strength, enough courage, or even enough faith to keep going. Doubt can be overwhelming, and it often strikes in our hardest times, making us question God's presence and provision. But the Bible is full of stories and promises that remind us God is our provider, always there to meet our needs, especially when we feel uncertain and afraid. The truth is, God understands our doubts and fears, and He meets us in those moments, giving us exactly what we need to press forward. One powerful verse that brings comfort is Philippians 4:19, which says, "But my God shall supply all your need according to his riches in glory by Christ Jesus." This verse reminds us that God's provision is endless, boundless, and exactly what we need, and it doesn't come from our strength or ability; it comes directly from Him. When we doubt, God doesn't turn away; instead, He steps in, showing us that His resources are infinite and that He is faithful to provide. Every time we're in need, God is already prepared to meet that need, whether it's physical, emotional, or spiritual, and His timing is always perfect, even if we can't see it at first. Provision in moments of doubt matters because it shows us that God is close to us, walking with us through every valley and over every hill, giving us hope that no matter what we face, we're never alone and we'll always have what we need in Him.

When we are in moments of doubt, it is easy to feel abandoned or like we have to face everything on our own, but God reassures us through His Word that He is our shepherd and we lack nothing with Him. In Psalm 23:1, David confidently declares, "The Lord is my shepherd; I shall not want." This verse captures a truth that's easy to forget when life feels overwhelming—that God is the shepherd who takes care of every need, guiding us, comforting us, and protecting us. When we feel like we're running out of answers, God is there, reminding us that His provision covers all our needs. He doesn't just give us barely enough; He gives us abundantly, and His provision is exactly what we need, exactly when we need it. Each time we doubt, God's promise in Psalm 23 reminds us to turn to Him, to rest in His care, and to believe that He will make a way, even if the path is unclear. Provision in moments of doubt strengthens our faith, showing us that God is always actively caring for us, even when we can't see what lies ahead.

Doubt also brings us to a place where we learn to rely not on ourselves, but on God's promises and His strength. In Isaiah 41:10, God speaks encouragement to His people, saying, "Fear thou not; for I am with thee: be not dismayed; for I am thy God: I will strengthen thee; yea, I will help thee; yea, I will uphold thee with the right hand of my righteousness." This verse is a reminder that God's presence is our anchor in times of doubt. He promises not only to be with us but to strengthen and uphold us, giving us what we need to keep moving forward, no matter how weak we feel. Our doubts and fears don't scare God away; they invite Him to show us how dependable His promises really are. Every time we feel weak, God is there, not to scold us, but to lift us up, to remind us that He is our strength. Provision in moments of doubt teaches us that God's help is constant, reliable, and unwavering, and that we can trust Him to carry us when we don't have the strength to carry ourselves.

The Bible also teaches us that God knows our needs even before we do and that He is always prepared to provide for us, even when we're unsure. In Matthew 6:31-33, Jesus speaks directly to our worries, saying, "Therefore take no thought, saying, What shall we eat? or, What shall we drink? or, Wherewithal shall we be clothed? (For after all these things do the Gentiles seek:) for your heavenly Father knoweth that ye have need of all these things. But seek ye first the kingdom of God, and his righteousness; and all these things shall be added unto you." This passage reminds us that God knows our needs intimately, and His provision is already set in place. Jesus invites us to trust in God, to prioritize our relationship with Him, and to believe that everything else we need will be taken care of. Provision in moments of doubt isn't just about having enough; it's about knowing that God is deeply aware of every detail of our lives, that He is attentive to our needs, and that His love is always working on our behalf. When we doubt, we're reminded to seek God first, to rest in His promises, and to know that He is always faithful to provide.

In moments of doubt, God's provision also comes through His peace, which guards our hearts and minds. In Philippians 4:6-7, we are encouraged, "Be careful for nothing; but in every thing by prayer and supplication with thanksgiving let your requests be made known unto God. And the peace of God, which passeth all understanding, shall keep your hearts and minds through Christ Jesus." This verse tells us that God's provision isn't just about physical needs; it's about the inner peace that comes when we bring our doubts and worries to Him. God's peace goes beyond our understanding, calming our hearts and giving us the strength to keep going. Each time we pray, God offers us His peace, showing us that even in moments of doubt, He is our refuge and our strength. This peace is a reminder that God is with us, that He hears us, and that His presence is enough to calm any storm we may face. Provision in moments of doubt means knowing that God's peace is always available, bringing calm and comfort to our hearts, helping us to trust that He is in control.

Finally, God's provision in doubt teaches us that He uses these moments to draw us closer to Him, strengthening our faith and reminding us of His constant love. In Deuteronomy 31:8, Moses encourages the Israelites, saying, "And the Lord, he it is that doth go before thee; he will be with thee, he will not fail thee, neither forsake thee: fear not, neither be dismayed." This verse reminds us that God is always with us, going before us, never leaving us alone. Doubt can make us feel isolated, but God's promise is that He will never forsake us. Every time we face moments of uncertainty, God is there, showing us that His love is steady, that His presence is unchanging, and that He will never leave us to figure things out on our own. Provision in moments of doubt reveals God's heart for us, showing us that His care is constant, that His support is sure, and that His love is the foundation we can stand on, no matter what we face.

In every moment of doubt, God's provision is a reminder of His faithfulness, His love, and His perfect timing. We may not always understand how God will provide, but we can trust that He sees every need, hears every prayer, and is always ready to meet us in our doubts. Provision in moments of doubt matters because it reminds us that God is our provider, that He is with us, and that we can trust Him completely. Through every challenge, every worry, and every uncertainty, God's provision gives us hope, showing us that we are never alone and that He will always be enough.

Day 22 - Patient Endurance Amidst Delays

In life, there are many times when things don't happen as quickly as we'd like, when doors seem to remain closed, and when we're left waiting for something we desperately want or need. These delays can be frustrating, leaving us feeling discouraged, anxious, or even hopeless as we wonder if our prayers are being heard. But the Bible teaches us that delays are not denials, and that in those moments of waiting, God is working in ways we cannot see, building our character, strengthening our faith, and teaching us lessons of patient endurance. Patient endurance is more than just waiting; it's about learning to trust in God's timing, believing in His promises, and finding hope in the knowledge that He is never late but always perfectly on time. In James 1:3-4, we read, "Knowing this, that the trying of your faith worketh patience. But let patience have her perfect work, that ye may be perfect and entire, wanting nothing." This powerful verse reminds us that the challenges we face in waiting are tools in God's hands, used to shape us, refine us, and make us complete. Through patient endurance, God is preparing us for the blessings and purposes He has planned, and each day we wait with faith, we are growing stronger, more resilient, and more like Christ. It matters to have hope in moments of frustration because God is always at work in the delays, teaching us lessons that will last a lifetime and showing us that His timing is always worth the wait.

One of the most precious lessons we learn through patient endurance is trust. In Proverbs 3:5-6, we are encouraged, "Trust in the Lord with all thine heart; and lean not unto thine own understanding. In all thy ways acknowledge him, and he shall direct thy paths." Waiting is often hard because we can't see what lies ahead, and we don't understand why things are taking so long. But through the waiting, God is teaching us to lean on Him, to put our full trust in His wisdom, and to believe that He knows what is best. Trusting God means letting go of our need to control everything, accepting that His ways are higher than ours, and believing that His timing is perfect. Patient endurance is like a school of trust, helping us to build our confidence in God's ability to lead us and reminding us that He is always in control, even when things don't make sense. This lesson of trust is a foundation that will carry us through life's ups and downs, grounding us in the knowledge that God is faithful, that He sees the bigger picture, and that He is always working for our good.

Through patient endurance, we also learn humility, recognizing that we are not the ones in charge and that we need God's guidance and strength to make it through. In 1 Peter 5:6, we read, "Humble yourselves therefore under the mighty hand of God, that he may exalt you in due time." This verse teaches us that humility is about surrendering to God's timing and trusting that He will lift us up when the time is right. Waiting humbles us, showing us that we don't have all the answers and that we need God's help in every part of our lives. Each day of patient endurance is a reminder to bow before God's wisdom, to accept His timing, and to trust that He knows what is best for us. Humility is a precious quality that grows in the soil of waiting, teaching us to depend on God, to let go of pride, and to find peace in the knowledge that He is guiding us. This lesson of humility helps us to approach life with open hands, ready to receive what God has in store, knowing that His timing is always perfect.

Another lesson we learn through patient endurance is resilience. In Romans 5:3-4, Paul writes, "And not only so, but we glory in tribulations also: knowing that tribulation worketh patience; And patience, experience; and experience, hope." This passage reminds us that patience, born from trials, leads to experience and ultimately to hope. Waiting is hard, but it builds resilience, teaching us to stay strong and to keep going even when things are difficult. Each time we choose to endure with faith, we are growing stronger, becoming more able to face life's challenges, and learning that we can trust God no matter what. Resilience is the ability to withstand hardships, to keep moving forward, and to hold onto hope even when the way is long. Through patient endurance, we are building a resilience that will carry us through future challenges, reminding us that with God by our side, we can face anything.

Patient endurance also teaches us gratitude, helping us to appreciate the blessings we may have overlooked. In 1 Thessalonians 5:18, we are encouraged, "In every thing give thanks: for this is the will of God in Christ Jesus concerning you." When we wait, we often become more aware of what we already have, learning to appreciate the small blessings and the simple moments. The waiting period becomes a time to focus on God's goodness, to count our blessings, and to be grateful for what He has already provided. This lesson of gratitude helps us to see life from a different perspective, to recognize the gifts we may have taken for granted, and to approach life with a heart of thankfulness. Patient endurance teaches us that every season, even the waiting season, is a gift, filled with opportunities to grow closer to God, to reflect on His love, and to be grateful for His faithfulness.

Perhaps one of the most powerful lessons of patient endurance is learning to hope in God's promises. In Isaiah 40:31, we are reminded, "But they that wait upon the Lord shall renew their strength; they shall mount up with wings as eagles; they shall run, and not be weary; and they shall walk, and not faint." This verse assures us that those who wait on God will find renewed strength and hope. Waiting is not passive; it is an active expression of faith, a way of holding onto God's promises even when we can't see the outcome. Each day of patient endurance is a day of hope, a day of believing that God's promises are true and that His plans are worth the wait. This hope is what keeps us going, lifting our hearts and giving us the strength to press forward, knowing that God is faithful and that He will fulfill His promises in His perfect timing. The lesson of hope is precious because it reminds us that with God, there is always a reason to keep going, always a future worth waiting for, and always a purpose in every delay.

In every season of waiting, God is teaching us precious lessons through patient endurance, shaping our character, strengthening our faith, and drawing us closer to Him. These lessons are gifts that will carry us through life, reminding us that God is with us, that His timing is perfect, and that His love is constant. Patient endurance is not just about getting through hard times; it's about growing, learning, and becoming more like Christ. Each moment of waiting is an opportunity to deepen our faith, to trust in God's promises, and to find joy in the journey. The lessons we learn through patient endurance are treasures that will last a lifetime, helping us to face life's challenges with courage, hope, and faith. In the end, we find that the waiting season was not a wasted season, but a time of growth, transformation, and discovery.

Day 23 - Pillars of Strength and Resilience

In life, we all face moments of struggle and frustration when things feel overwhelming, when hope seems faint, and when the challenges before us feel impossible to overcome. These hard times test our strength and resilience, making us question whether we have what it takes to keep going. But the Bible teaches us that even in our weakest moments, God is there to make us stronger, giving us the strength and resilience we need to face each day. God becomes our pillar, our foundation, our rock, and He invites us to lean on Him so we can stand firm no matter what life throws at us. In Isaiah 41:10, God encourages us with these words: "Fear thou not; for I am with thee: be not dismayed; for I am thy God: I will strengthen thee; yea, I will help thee; yea, I will uphold thee with the right hand of my righteousness." This promise reminds us that God's strength is greater than any challenge we face, and His support is always there for us. God doesn't just give us strength; He becomes our strength, offering His powerful hand to hold us up, carry us through, and help us keep going. The idea of God being our pillar of strength and resilience is incredibly important because it gives us hope, reminding us that we are not alone in our struggles and that we don't have to rely solely on our own strength.

One of the reasons why these pillars of strength and resilience are so crucial is because they teach us to rely on God rather than ourselves. When we face difficulties, it's easy to feel like we have to handle everything on our own, to carry all our burdens without asking for help. But God reminds us over and over again that He is there for us, inviting us to lean on Him, to give Him our worries, and to trust that He will carry us through. In Psalm 55:22, we are encouraged, "Cast thy burden upon the Lord, and he shall sustain thee: he shall never suffer the righteous to be moved." This verse teaches us that God wants to carry our burdens, to take our worries and replace them with His peace. Each time we choose to lean on God's strength, we are reminded that we don't have to face life's struggles alone, that God is our rock, our fortress, and our safe place. By learning to rely on Him, we find a strength that goes beyond our own, a resilience that can withstand any storm, and a peace that calms our hearts even in the hardest times.

Through God, we also find resilience—the ability to bounce back, to keep moving forward, and to rise above our challenges. In 2 Corinthians 4:8-9, Paul writes, "We are troubled on every side, yet not distressed; we are perplexed, but not in despair; Persecuted, but not forsaken; cast down, but not destroyed." This powerful message reminds us that with God, we can face trials without being defeated. Resilience doesn't mean that life will be easy or that we won't face hard times, but it means that, through God's strength, we can withstand whatever comes our way. Resilience is a gift from God, a quality that grows each time we choose to stand firm in faith, to trust in God's promises, and to believe that He is working all things together for our good. When we face setbacks, failures, or disappointments, resilience reminds us that we can get back up, that God is still with us, and that His plan is greater than any temporary struggle. This resilience is one of the most valuable pillars of faith, showing us that we are never defeated as long as we hold onto God's hand.

Another reason why strength and resilience matter is that they enable us to be a source of hope and encouragement for others. When we face challenges and find strength in God, we become a testimony to His faithfulness, a living example of His power to overcome. In 2 Corinthians 1:3-4, we read, "Blessed be God, even the Father of our Lord Jesus Christ, the Father of mercies, and the God of all comfort; Who comforteth us in all our tribulation, that we may be able to comfort them which are in any trouble, by the comfort wherewith we ourselves are comforted of God." This verse shows us that God comforts us not only for our own sake but so that we can offer that same comfort to others. Each time we experience God's strength and resilience in our lives, we are better equipped to support those around us, to encourage others who may be struggling, and to show them that God is their pillar, too. Our strength becomes a blessing to others, a source of hope, and a reminder that God's power is available to everyone who calls upon Him. By standing strong, we inspire others to do the same, showing them that with God, anything is possible.

Resilience also builds perseverance, helping us to keep going even when things seem hopeless. In James 1:12, we are reminded, "Blessed is the man that endureth temptation: for when he is tried, he shall receive the crown of life, which the Lord hath promised to them that love him." This verse tells us that perseverance is rewarded, that each time we endure with faith, we are moving closer to the blessings God has promised. Perseverance is a quality that develops over time, growing each time we choose to trust God, to keep believing, and to press on even when we're tired or discouraged. With God's strength, we find the courage to persevere, to hold onto hope, and to believe that better days are ahead. This perseverance is a pillar that keeps us steady, helping us to stay the course, to finish the race, and to hold onto God's promises no matter what. Through perseverance, we grow stronger, more determined, and more grounded in our faith, discovering that with God, we have the power to endure anything.

Finally, the pillars of strength and resilience help us to keep our focus on God's eternal promises rather than on temporary struggles. In 2 Corinthians 4:17-18, Paul encourages us, "For our light affliction, which is but for a moment, worketh for us a far more exceeding and eternal weight of glory; While we look not at the things which are seen, but at the things which are not seen: for the things which are seen are temporal; but the things which are not seen are eternal." This passage reminds us that our struggles are temporary, but the strength and resilience we build through them have eternal value. Each time we face a challenge with faith, we are investing in something greater than ourselves, something that will last forever. The pillars of strength and resilience help us to look beyond the present moment, to focus on God's promises, and to find hope in the knowledge that our struggles are preparing us for something far greater. This eternal perspective gives us courage, helping us to endure with faith, to trust in God's plan, and to know that every challenge we face has a purpose.

In every season of life, God is our pillar of strength and resilience, offering us His support, His guidance, and His unchanging love. These pillars are the foundation that holds us steady, the strength that carries us through, and the hope that lifts our spirits even in the darkest times. By leaning on God, we find a strength that goes beyond our own, a resilience that cannot be shaken, and a peace that surpasses all understanding. The pillars of strength and resilience remind us that we are not alone, that God is with us, and that we can face any challenge with courage and faith.

Day 24 - Promises Kept in the Dark Times

In life, we all go through dark times, seasons of struggle, loss, or frustration when it feels like the light is far away and hope is hard to hold onto. These are the moments when doubt creeps in, when we wonder if things will ever get better, and when it feels like our prayers go unheard. But the Bible assures us that even in our darkest times, God is still with us, and He keeps His promises. God's Word is full of promises made by a loving and faithful Father who has never failed and never will. Even when we can't see how things will improve or how the future will unfold, we can find hope in knowing that God's promises are unbreakable. In Deuteronomy 31:8, we are comforted with these words: "And the Lord, he it is that doth go before thee; he will be with thee, he will not fail thee, neither forsake thee: fear not, neither be dismayed." This verse reminds us that God is already ahead of us, preparing the way, and that He will never leave us alone. In times of darkness, God's promises become a source of strength, reminding us that we are not forgotten and that He is always by our side. It matters to hold onto these promises because they give us hope, even when everything around us feels uncertain or hopeless. God's promises are a light in our darkest moments, showing us that He is working behind the scenes and that His plans for us are always good.

One of the reasons why promises kept in dark times are so important is that they remind us of God's unchanging nature. While life is full of change and uncertainty, God's character remains the same yesterday, today, and forever. In Numbers 23:19, we read, "God is not a man, that he should lie; neither the son of man, that he should repent: hath he said, and shall he not do it? or hath he spoken, and shall he not make it good?" This verse reassures us that God is faithful and true to His Word, unlike people who may break their promises. Every promise God makes is a promise He keeps. When we're facing dark times, remembering God's faithfulness helps us to trust that He will bring us through, that He will keep every promise, and that His love for us is steadfast. Knowing that God's promises are sure gives us something solid to hold onto, an anchor that keeps us steady when the storms of life try to shake our faith.

Dark times also teach us to rely on God's promises in ways we may not have before. When things are going well, it's easy to take God's Word for granted, but in our lowest moments, His promises become a lifeline. In Psalm 46:1, we are reminded, "God is our refuge and strength, a very present help in trouble." This verse shows us that God's promises are not distant or far off; they are here for us right now, meeting us in our struggles and giving us the strength to keep going. God promises to be our refuge, a safe place where we can find rest and hope. Each time we turn to Him in the dark, we find that His promises are real, that His presence is near, and that His strength is enough for whatever we're facing. Holding onto God's promises during tough times builds our faith, teaching us to rely on Him more deeply and helping us to experience His love and comfort in new ways.

In dark times, God's promises also remind us that He has a plan for us, a future filled with hope. In Jeremiah 29:11, God speaks these encouraging words to His people: "For I know the thoughts that I think toward you, saith the Lord, thoughts of peace, and not of evil, to give you an expected end." This verse tells us that God's plans for us are good, even when we can't see it. He knows the future, and He is guiding us toward it with love and wisdom. When life feels overwhelming, holding onto this promise gives us the courage to trust that God is in control, that He has a purpose for our struggles, and that He is leading us to a place of peace and blessing. God's promises give us hope for tomorrow, showing us that our current pain is not the end of the story, that He is working everything together for good, and that His plans are filled with peace.

God's promises in dark times also help us to remember that we are never alone. In Isaiah 41:10, God speaks directly to our fears, saying, "Fear thou not; for I am with thee: be not dismayed; for I am thy God: I will strengthen thee; yea, I will help thee; yea, I will uphold thee with the right hand of my righteousness." This verse reminds us that God is right by our side, ready to help us, support us, and lift us up. In our hardest moments, it's easy to feel isolated or abandoned, but God promises to be with us, to carry us when we're too weak to go on, and to give us the strength we need. His presence becomes our comfort, His promises become our security, and His love becomes our reason to keep going. Knowing that God is with us, that He will never leave or forsake us, helps us to face each day with courage, no matter how dark it may seem.

God's promises also bring us peace that surpasses understanding. In Philippians 4:6-7, we are encouraged, "Be careful for nothing; but in every thing by prayer and supplication with thanksgiving let your requests be made known unto God. And the peace of God, which passeth all understanding, shall keep your hearts and minds through Christ Jesus." This passage tells us that even in dark times, we can experience a peace that doesn't depend on our circumstances. God promises to guard our hearts and minds with His peace when we bring our worries to Him. This peace is a gift that helps us to rest, to let go of our fears, and to trust that God is in control. Holding onto God's promises brings us this peace, a calm assurance that He is working in our lives and that everything will be okay, even when we don't understand how. God's promises are like a shield, protecting us from despair and helping us to stay steady, even when life feels chaotic.

Finally, God's promises in dark times teach us to have hope and to look forward to the blessings He has prepared for us. In Romans 8:18, Paul encourages us with these words: "For I reckon that the sufferings of this present time are not worthy to be compared with the glory which shall be revealed in us." This verse reminds us that our struggles are temporary and that God has something far greater waiting for us. Each time we hold onto God's promises, we are reminded that our pain is not the end and that God's blessings are coming. This hope is what keeps us moving forward, what lifts our spirits, and what reminds us that God's promises are true. With God, every dark time has a purpose, every struggle brings us closer to Him, and every tear will one day be wiped away.

Day 25 - Prioritizing Faith Over Frustration

In life, we all face moments of frustration, when things don't go as planned, when obstacles seem to block our every step, and when it feels like we're stuck in a cycle of disappointment. It's easy to let frustration take over, to feel overwhelmed and defeated. But the Bible teaches us something powerful: in these moments, we can choose to prioritize faith over frustration, to lean into our trust in God even when the way forward seems impossible. Choosing faith means deciding to see our challenges as opportunities for God to show His power, to guide us, and to strengthen us. In 2 Corinthians 5:7, we are reminded, "For we walk by faith, not by sight." This verse encourages us to look beyond what we can see with our eyes and instead to trust in what God has promised, to believe that He is working, even if we don't understand His plan right now. Prioritizing faith over frustration is a choice we make in every difficult moment, a decision to believe that God is greater than any problem we face and that His promises are true. This matters because it gives us hope, reminding us that no matter how tough things get, we are never alone and we are never without help. Faith lifts us up, giving us strength to keep going, even when frustration would have us give up. It's a reminder that God is with us, that He's fighting for us, and that He will make a way where there seems to be none.

One of the reasons it's so important to prioritize faith over frustration is that it keeps our focus on God rather than on our circumstances. When we allow frustration to take over, we start to focus on what's wrong, on what we can't change, and on what we lack. But faith shifts our perspective, helping us to see that God is bigger than any obstacle and that He is fully capable of turning things around. In Philippians 4:6-7, we are encouraged, "Be careful for nothing; but in every thing by prayer and supplication with thanksgiving let your requests be made known unto God. And the peace of God, which passeth all understanding, shall keep your hearts and minds through Christ Jesus." This passage reminds us that faith is about bringing our concerns to God, trusting that He will handle them, and letting His peace fill our hearts. Instead of letting frustration lead us into worry and doubt, faith invites us to bring everything to God in prayer, to trust that He hears us, and to let go of the need to control every outcome. This kind of faith-filled focus keeps us steady, helping us to stay calm in the face of challenges and to remember that God is in control, no matter how chaotic things may seem.

Prioritizing faith over frustration also builds patience within us, teaching us to wait on God's timing rather than trying to force things to happen on our own. In James 1:3-4, we read, "Knowing this, that the trying of your faith worketh patience. But let patience have her perfect work, that ye may be perfect and entire, wanting nothing." This verse shows us that challenges are opportunities for growth, helping us to develop patience and to trust in God's timing. Frustration often arises because we want things to happen right away, but faith reminds us that God's timing is perfect, that He sees the bigger picture, and that He is working all things together for our good. Each time we choose faith over frustration, we are learning to wait on God, to be patient, and to trust that He knows exactly when and how to bring about the best results. This patience becomes a strength that carries us through future challenges, teaching us to rely on God's wisdom rather than our own.

Faith over frustration also strengthens our resilience, helping us to persevere through hard times without losing hope. In Galatians 6:9, we are encouraged, "And let us not be weary in well doing: for in due season we shall reap, if we faint not." This verse reminds us that our efforts are not in vain, that every act of faith, every prayer, and every step forward matters. Frustration can make us feel like giving up, but faith reminds us that God honors our perseverance, that He sees our struggles, and that He promises a reward for those who keep going. Resilience is the ability to keep moving forward, to trust in God's promises, and to believe that He will bring us through, no matter how tough things may get. Each time we choose faith over frustration, we are building resilience, becoming stronger in our trust in God, and finding the courage to face whatever comes our way.

Another reason to prioritize faith over frustration is that it helps us to stay connected to God's promises, even when life feels uncertain. In Hebrews 11:1, we are told, "Now faith is the substance of things hoped for, the evidence of things not seen." Faith is about holding onto what God has promised, even when we can't see the outcome. Frustration makes us focus on what's not working, but faith invites us to focus on what God has said, to remember His promises, and to trust that He will bring them to pass. This connection to God's promises gives us hope, helping us to look beyond the present moment and to believe that God has a plan for our future. Prioritizing faith over frustration means choosing to believe that God's promises are true, that His plans are good, and that He is faithful to do what He has said. This hope keeps us anchored, giving us a reason to keep going, even when the way is hard.

Finally, choosing faith over frustration helps us to be a light to others, showing them the power of trusting in God. When we respond to challenges with faith rather than frustration, we become examples of God's love, peace, and strength. In Matthew 5:16, Jesus encourages us, "Let your light so shine before men, that they may see your good works, and glorify your Father which is in heaven." By choosing faith, we are showing others that God is real, that His promises are true, and that He is always with us. Our faith-filled response to frustration becomes a testimony, a way of pointing others to God and helping them to see that they too can find hope in Him. Each time we choose faith, we are sharing God's love with the world, showing them that even in difficult times, there is a source of peace and strength available to them.

In every moment of frustration, prioritizing faith over frustration reminds us that God is greater than any problem, that His promises are true, and that His love is constant. Faith lifts us up, gives us hope, and helps us to see beyond our current struggles.

Day 26 - Powerful Lessons from Small Wins

In life, we often look for big breakthroughs, major victories, or drastic changes to find hope and feel fulfilled. However, the Bible shows us that some of the most powerful lessons come from small wins, those little moments of progress that may seem minor but actually carry immense value. These small wins are reminders from God that He is working in our lives, even in ways we might not notice immediately. When we see little steps forward, it's as if God is whispering, "I am here, guiding you, and I'm with you in every step you take." In Zechariah 4:10, we're reminded, "For who hath despised the day of small things?" This verse teaches us that even the small beginnings and tiny victories have a purpose. Small wins, whether they are moments of unexpected joy, answered prayers, or times when we choose to trust God a little more, help build our faith, teach us patience, and remind us to find joy in every step of our journey. Powerful lessons from small wins matter because they reveal that God is involved in every detail of our lives and that every bit of progress is worth celebrating. When we look at life through the lens of faith, we see that each small win is like a piece of a larger puzzle, building a bigger picture that God has planned for us.

One of the biggest lessons small wins teach us is gratitude. When we begin to notice and appreciate the small victories, our hearts open to thankfulness, realizing that God's blessings are around us every day. In 1 Thessalonians 5:18, we are instructed, "In every thing give thanks: for this is the will of God in Christ Jesus concerning you." Gratitude shifts our focus from what we don't have to what God has already provided, helping us to recognize His hand in our lives. Each small win reminds us to thank God, to appreciate the good, and to see that even on the toughest days, He is giving us reasons to smile and hold on to hope. Gratitude becomes a habit, a way of looking at life that fills us with joy and helps us find strength even in difficult times. This lesson of gratitude is powerful because it changes our perspective, showing us that there is beauty and hope in every moment.

Another lesson from small wins is the importance of patience. Life doesn't always move as quickly as we'd like, and sometimes, progress seems slow. But small wins remind us that even if things aren't happening all at once, God is still moving. In James 1:3-4, we are told, "Knowing this, that the trying of your faith worketh patience. But let patience have her perfect work, that ye may be perfect and entire, wanting nothing." Small victories teach us to value patience, showing us that growth and change often happen little by little. Patience is about trusting in God's timing, knowing that He is building something good in us. Each small win is a stepping stone, helping us to grow and reminding us that we are on a journey. This lesson of patience is powerful because it helps us to remain calm, hopeful, and focused on God, even when life doesn't look exactly how we want it to. Through patience, we learn to trust that every small win is part of a bigger picture, a plan that God is carefully unfolding in His perfect time.

Small wins also teach us resilience, the strength to keep going even when things are hard. Sometimes, we face setbacks, but each small win is like a light that encourages us to push forward, reminding us that we are making progress. In Galatians 6:9, we are encouraged, "And let us not be weary in well doing: for in due season we shall reap, if we faint not." This verse reassures us that our efforts matter and that we are on the path to something greater. Small wins are like little rewards, helping us to stay motivated and to believe that God is with us. They remind us that we are capable, that we can overcome challenges, and that with God's help, every effort counts. The lesson of resilience is powerful because it keeps us strong, showing us that we are not defined by failures but by our ability to get back up and try again. Each small victory builds our confidence, strengthens our faith, and helps us to move forward, step by step.

Small wins also help us recognize the value of consistency, of staying faithful in the little things. It can be tempting to focus only on big goals, but small wins remind us that daily faithfulness is important too. In Luke 16:10, Jesus teaches, "He that is faithful in that which is least is faithful also in much." This verse shows us that God values our dedication in the small tasks, that He sees our efforts, and that He honors those who remain faithful in every season. When we celebrate small wins, we are reminded to keep showing up, to keep doing our best, and to trust that God notices even the smallest acts of faith. Consistency matters because it builds character, helping us to become people who are reliable, trustworthy, and committed. Each small win is a reminder that we are growing, that we are getting better, and that God is pleased with our efforts, no matter how small they may seem.

Another powerful lesson we learn from small wins is hope. Each small victory, each little bit of progress, reminds us that God is at work in our lives and that things are moving forward, even if it's in tiny steps. In Romans 15:13, we read, "Now the God of hope fill you with all joy and peace in believing, that ye may abound in hope, through the power of the Holy Ghost." Hope is what keeps us going, what lifts our spirits, and what reminds us that with God, nothing is impossible. Small wins fuel our hope, giving us glimpses of what God is doing and encouraging us to trust in His plans. Each small victory is a reason to keep believing, to keep praying, and to keep hoping for greater things. The lesson of hope is powerful because it reminds us that no matter how dark things may seem, there is always a reason to believe in a brighter future.

Finally, small wins teach us to lean on God for every need, big or small. In John 15:5, Jesus says, "I am the vine, ye are the branches: He that abideth in me, and I in him, the same bringeth forth much fruit: for without me ye can do nothing." This verse shows us that our strength comes from staying connected to God, that every victory is a result of His presence in our lives. Small wins remind us to turn to God in every moment, to thank Him for each blessing, and to rely on His strength. They teach us that we don't have to do everything on our own and that God cares about every detail. This dependence on God is powerful because it keeps us grounded, helping us to remember that He is our source of strength, joy, and peace. Each small win is a reminder that with God, we can overcome anything and that His grace is enough for every moment.

In every moment of life, powerful lessons from small wins show us that God is working, that He is with us, and that He is guiding us on a journey of growth, faith, and hope. Each small victory is a reason to celebrate, to thank God, and to believe that He is doing great things in our lives. The lessons we learn from these small wins shape our hearts, strengthen our faith, and remind us that God's love and guidance are with us every step of the way.

Day 27 - Persistence Beyond Visible Progress

IN LIFE, WE OFTEN FACE times when it feels like all our efforts lead to nothing, like we're trying our hardest yet seeing no results, and it can be incredibly discouraging. Moments of frustration are difficult to bear, especially when we want to move forward, yet progress seems invisible. However, the Bible encourages us to keep going, to have faith even when we can't see the fruits of our labor, to trust that God is working behind the scenes in ways we don't understand. God calls us to persistence, a steady commitment to continue moving forward even when progress isn't obvious. Galatians 6:9 speaks powerfully to this, saying, "And let us not be weary in well doing: for in due season we shall reap, if we faint not." This verse reminds us that our efforts are never wasted, even if we can't see results right away. It takes faith to keep going, to persist even when we feel tired or overlooked, but God promises that there is a harvest waiting for those who don't give up. Persistence beyond visible progress matters because it deepens our faith, teaches us patience, and reminds us that God's timing is perfect. Each step we take without seeing results is an act of trust, a way of saying, "God, I believe You are working, even if I don't see it yet." And it's in those steps of trust that we grow, finding strength and resilience we didn't know we had.

One reason persistence matters so much is that it builds character, shaping us into people who rely on God rather than on what we can control or see. In James 1:2-4, we're encouraged, "My brethren, count it all joy when ye fall into divers temptations; Knowing this, that the trying of your faith worketh patience. But let patience have her perfect work, that ye may be perfect and entire, wanting nothing." Patience and persistence are closely tied, as both require us to keep going and trust that God's work is happening, even when we don't see it. Every moment we choose persistence over giving up is a moment of growth, a way of letting God work within us to build a faith that doesn't rely on immediate results. This kind of faith is strong and unshakeable because it is rooted in God's promises rather than our own understanding. The character we develop through persistence makes us resilient, giving us the ability to stand firm in faith no matter what life throws our way.

Persistence beyond visible progress also reminds us to keep our focus on God rather than on what we lack. In Philippians 4:13, Paul writes, "I can do all things through Christ which strengtheneth me." This verse is a reminder that our strength comes from God, not from ourselves or from what we can see. When we feel like we're making no progress, it's easy to feel weak or discouraged, but God's strength is made perfect in our weakness. He fills the gaps where we fall short, giving us the ability to keep going. Each step forward, even when we don't see immediate results, is a step taken in God's strength. Persistence teaches us to lean on Him, to trust that He is the one sustaining us, and to remember that He is always with us, helping us to keep moving forward. This dependence on God's strength keeps us grounded, reminding us that we don't have to carry everything on our own and that God's power is enough for whatever challenges we face.

In moments when progress feels invisible, persistence also brings us closer to God, deepening our relationship with Him. In Isaiah 40:31, we read, "But they that wait upon the Lord shall renew their strength; they shall mount up with wings as eagles; they shall run, and not be weary; and they shall walk, and not faint." Waiting on God, pressing on even when we don't see results, draws us nearer to Him. Each day we choose to persist is a day we spend trusting in His promises, learning to rely on His faithfulness rather than on our own abilities. Persistence teaches us to pray, to seek God's guidance, and to find comfort in His presence. Through this, we become more in tune with God's voice, more aware of His presence, and more confident in His love for us. This closeness to God strengthens us in ways we may not realize at first, giving us the courage to face each day with faith and hope, even when progress is unseen.

Another powerful aspect of persistence is that it teaches us humility. In our world, we're often focused on results, on achieving something visible, but God's perspective is different. In Proverbs 3:5-6, we're instructed, "Trust in the Lord with all thine heart; and lean not unto thine own understanding. In all thy ways acknowledge him, and he shall direct thy paths." Choosing to persist without seeing progress requires us to let go of our desire for control, to trust in God's understanding rather than our own. It humbles us, reminding us that we don't have to know every answer or see every step ahead, and that God's ways are higher than ours. Humility opens our hearts to God's will, helping us to accept that His timing is better than our own and that every act of persistence, no matter how small, is valuable in His eyes. This humility frees us from the pressure to prove ourselves, allowing us to find peace in simply following God's lead, trusting that He will guide us exactly where we need to be.

Persistence beyond visible progress also keeps hope alive, reminding us that with God, nothing is impossible. In Romans 8:28, we read, "And we know that all things work together for good to them that love God, to them who are the called according to his purpose." This verse assures us that God is working all things for good, even when we can't see it yet. Every step of persistence is a step of hope, a way of holding onto the belief that God is working behind the scenes, arranging things for our good. Hope is what keeps us going, what lifts our spirits, and what reminds us that God's plans are greater than anything we can imagine. Each time we choose to persist, we are choosing hope, believing that there is a purpose in our journey and that God's promises are true. This hope becomes a light that guides us, helping us to see beyond the present moment and to trust that God's blessings are coming, even if they are not visible right now.

Finally, persistence beyond visible progress allows us to be a source of encouragement to others. When we choose to keep going despite challenges, we become an example of faith, a reminder to those around us that God's strength is real and that His promises are worth holding onto. In Matthew 5:16, Jesus encourages us, "Let your light so shine before men, that they may see your good works, and glorify your Father which is in heaven." By persisting, we let our light shine, showing others that faith is not about immediate results but about trusting God's plan. Our persistence can inspire others to keep going, to believe that with God, all things are possible, and to find hope in their own journey. We become a living testimony of God's faithfulness, a reminder that He is with us every step of the way and that He honors those who continue in faith.

In every moment of life, persistence beyond visible progress matters because it builds our faith, strengthens our character, and draws us closer to God. Each step of persistence is a declaration of trust, a choice to believe in God's promises, and a reminder that with Him, we are never alone.

Day 28 - Potential Unlocked Through Patience

In life, we often find ourselves eager for things to change, wanting answers to our prayers right away, and hoping for quick solutions to our problems. It's natural to wish for progress and growth, especially when we're facing hard times and feeling frustrated. But the Bible shows us that sometimes the most beautiful things in life take time to develop, and that patience is the key to unlocking the full potential that God has placed within us. Patience is not just about waiting; it's about learning to trust God's timing and believing that He knows what's best for us. In James 1:4, we read, "But let patience have her perfect work, that ye may be perfect and entire, wanting nothing." This verse reminds us that patience is part of God's process for making us whole, for helping us reach our fullest potential. When we let patience do its work, we are shaped and strengthened, and our faith deepens in ways we could never have imagined. Potential unlocked through patience matters because it transforms us, teaching us to rely on God, to grow through our challenges, and to find hope even when we can't see the outcome right away. Patience is God's way of preparing us for the blessings He has in store, reminding us that every season of waiting is a season of growth.

One of the greatest lessons patience teaches us is to trust in God's plan. In Proverbs 3:5-6, we are encouraged, "Trust in the Lord with all thine heart; and lean not unto thine own understanding. In all thy ways acknowledge him, and he shall direct thy paths." Patience requires us to let go of our desire to control everything and to trust that God is guiding us, even when we don't see immediate results. Trusting God means believing that He has a purpose for every delay and that He is working all things together for our good. Each moment of patience helps us to build this trust, reminding us that God's timing is perfect and that His plan is greater than our own. This trust becomes the foundation of our faith, allowing us to face challenges with confidence, knowing that God is in control. Patience unlocks our potential by teaching us to rely on God, to surrender our worries, and to believe that He is leading us in the right direction.

Patience also teaches us resilience, the ability to keep going even when things are hard. In Romans 5:3-4, Paul writes, "And not only so, but we glory in tribulations also: knowing that tribulation worketh patience; And patience, experience; and experience, hope." This passage shows us that patience is born from challenges and that each difficulty we face strengthens us, helping us to become more resilient. Resilience is the strength to keep moving forward, to trust in God's promises, and to believe that He is with us every step of the way. Patience helps us to build this resilience, showing us that even the longest journeys are made one step at a time. Each time we choose patience over frustration, we are growing stronger, becoming more able to handle life's challenges, and learning to trust that God's grace is enough. This resilience becomes a powerful part of our character, a reminder that with God, we have the strength to overcome any obstacle and that every delay is an opportunity for growth.

Another reason why patience is so important is that it helps us to see the bigger picture, to look beyond our immediate desires and to focus on God's greater purpose for our lives. In Isaiah 40:31, we read, "But they that wait upon the Lord shall renew their strength; they shall mount up with wings as eagles; they shall run, and not be weary; and they shall walk, and not faint." This verse reminds us that waiting on God renews our strength, that patience is not wasted time but time spent growing closer to God. Each moment of patience allows us to pause, to reflect, and to see life from God's perspective. Patience unlocks our potential by helping us to focus on what truly matters, to see that God's plans are higher than our own, and to trust that He is leading us toward something beautiful. When we embrace patience, we find peace in the journey, knowing that God is working behind the scenes and that every delay has a purpose.

Through patience, we also learn humility, recognizing that we don't have all the answers and that we need God's wisdom and guidance. In 1 Peter 5:6, we are reminded, "Humble yourselves therefore under the mighty hand of God, that he may exalt you in due time." This verse teaches us that patience is a form of humility, a way of saying, "God, I trust You to lead me, even if I don't understand everything right now." Patience helps us to let go of our pride, to stop trying to force our own plans, and to allow God to work in His way and in His time. This humility opens our hearts to God's will, helping us to become more willing to follow His guidance and to trust that His timing is perfect. Humility becomes a source of strength, showing us that we don't have to have everything figured out, that we can rest in God's wisdom, and that His plans are always for our good. Patience unlocks our potential by teaching us to lean on God, to trust His timing, and to allow His grace to shape our lives.

Patience also brings us closer to God, helping us to build a deeper relationship with Him. In Psalm 27:14, we are encouraged, "Wait on the Lord: be of good courage, and he shall strengthen thine heart: wait, I say, on the Lord." Waiting on God teaches us to seek Him, to spend time in His presence, and to find strength in His love. Each moment of patience is a moment of connection with God, a chance to pray, to listen, and to grow closer to Him. This closeness to God fills us with peace, reminding us that we are never alone and that He is always with us, guiding us through every season of life. Patience unlocks our potential by helping us to become more connected to God, to rely on His strength, and to trust in His love. As we wait on Him, we find that our faith grows, that our hearts are filled with hope, and that we are more equipped to face whatever comes our way.

Finally, patience gives us hope, showing us that with God, there is always a reason to keep going. In Romans 8:25, we are reminded, "But if we hope for that we see not, then do we with patience wait for it." This verse teaches us that patience and hope go hand in hand, that each moment of waiting is a moment of hope, a chance to believe that God's promises are true. Patience unlocks our potential by helping us to hold onto hope, to believe that God is working in our lives, and to trust that His blessings are on the way. Each day we choose patience, we are choosing hope, choosing to believe that God's timing is perfect, and that His plans are worth the wait.

In every season of life, potential unlocked through patience shows us that God is with us, that He is guiding us, and that He is helping us to become the people He created us to be. Patience matters because it teaches us to trust in God's timing, to find strength in His promises, and to believe that every delay has a purpose. Through patience, we learn to rely on God, to grow in faith, and to find joy in the journey. The lessons we learn from patience shape our hearts, strengthen our character, and remind us that with God, we can unlock our full potential and live a life filled with purpose and hope.

Day 29 - Proof That the Journey Matters

In life, it's easy to get caught up in the desire to reach our goals quickly, to achieve success, and to see results right away. When we're facing moments of frustration, it's natural to feel impatient, to wonder why things aren't happening faster, and to question if all our efforts even matter. But the Bible teaches us that the journey itself—the steps we take, the lessons we learn along the way, and the ways we grow through both good and hard times—is deeply important and has its own purpose. The journey matters because it shapes us, strengthens us, and brings us closer to God. Each experience, whether it feels like a win or a setback, is part of the plan God has for our lives. In Romans 5:3-4, we read, "And not only so, but we glory in tribulations also: knowing that tribulation worketh patience; And patience, experience; and experience, hope." This verse reminds us that the challenges we face along the journey are not obstacles but opportunities for growth. They build patience in us, which in turn gives us experience, and that experience fills us with hope. Proof that the journey matters can be seen in the way God uses each step to prepare us for what's ahead, teaching us to trust Him, helping us to become more resilient, and allowing us to see His presence in every season of our lives. Moments of frustration may tempt us to give up, but if we trust that the journey has meaning, we find hope, knowing that every part of it is leading us closer to the person God created us to be.

One of the most powerful reasons the journey matters is that it teaches us to depend on God rather than on ourselves. In Proverbs 3:5-6, we are encouraged, "Trust in the Lord with all thine heart; and lean not unto thine own understanding. In all thy ways acknowledge him, and he shall direct thy paths." Life's journey often brings us to places we don't understand, and we may face situations where we feel lost or unsure of what to do next. But through these moments, we learn that we don't have to know everything or be able to control every outcome. Instead, we are invited to trust in God's wisdom, to lean on His guidance, and to believe that He is leading us exactly where we need to be. Each step we take in faith, especially when we're frustrated or uncertain, is a step of trust, a way of saying, "God, I believe that You have a plan for me." This trust is essential because it draws us closer to God, teaching us to rely on

His strength and to find peace in His presence. The journey matters because it shows us that we are not alone and that God is with us, guiding us every step of the way.

The journey also builds our character, helping us to become stronger, kinder, and more compassionate. In James 1:2-4, we are reminded, "My brethren, count it all joy when ye fall into divers temptations; Knowing this, that the trying of your faith worketh patience. But let patience have her perfect work, that ye may be perfect and entire, wanting nothing." This verse teaches us that challenges are not just things to be endured but are opportunities for growth. They refine us, helping us to develop patience, resilience, and a deeper understanding of ourselves and others. The journey matters because it shapes who we are, molding our character and helping us to reflect the love and grace of God. Through every trial and triumph, we are learning to become more like Christ, to love more deeply, and to live with purpose. The character we build along the journey becomes a lasting part of us, a source of strength that carries us through future challenges and allows us to be a blessing to others.

Along the journey, we also learn to find joy in the little things, to appreciate the blessings that God gives us each day. In 1 Thessalonians 5:18, we are encouraged, "In every thing give thanks: for this is the will of God in Christ Jesus concerning you." This verse reminds us to cultivate gratitude, to find joy in each step, and to see God's hand in the small moments. Frustration often tempts us to focus on what we don't have or what hasn't happened yet, but gratitude shifts our perspective, helping us to recognize the beauty and goodness around us. The journey matters because it teaches us to live in the present, to cherish each day, and to see that every moment is a gift. When we learn to appreciate the journey, we find that life is full of blessings, even in the midst of difficulties, and that God's love and grace are always present.

Another reason the journey matters is that it allows us to witness God's faithfulness in every season. In Deuteronomy 31:8, we find comfort in these words: "And the Lord, he it is that doth go before thee; he will be with thee, he will not fail thee, neither forsake thee: fear not, neither be dismayed." Throughout the journey of life, we face both joys and sorrows, but through it all, God remains with us, guiding us, comforting us, and helping us to keep moving forward. Each challenge we overcome and each moment of joy we experience is proof of God's faithfulness. The journey matters because it shows us that God is always there, that He never leaves us, and that His promises are true. When we look back on the journey, we see how God has carried us through, how He has answered prayers, and how He has provided for us in ways we may not have expected. This reminder of God's faithfulness gives us hope, helping us to trust that He will continue to be with us in every step ahead.

The journey also gives us the opportunity to build meaningful connections with others, to support each other, and to share God's love. In Hebrews 10:24-25, we are encouraged, "And let us consider one another to provoke unto love and to good works: Not forsaking the assembling of ourselves together, as the manner of some is; but exhorting one another." Along life's journey, we meet people who encourage us, who walk with us through hard times, and who remind us that we are not alone. We also become sources of encouragement for others, sharing our experiences, offering comfort, and helping them to see God's goodness. The journey matters because it connects us to others, allowing us to grow together, to lift each other up, and to share in the joy and strength that come from community. These relationships are gifts, reminders of God's love, and sources of hope that carry us through life's challenges.

Finally, the journey teaches us patience and hope, showing us that God's timing is perfect and that His plans are worth the wait. In Romans 8:25, we read, "But if we hope for that we see not, then do we with patience wait for it." This verse reminds us that hope is often unseen, that it requires patience, and that God's blessings come in His perfect time. Each step of the journey, especially the difficult ones, teaches us to wait on God, to trust that He knows what's best, and to believe that His promises are true. The journey matters because it builds our hope, helping us to look forward to the future with faith and to believe that God has good things in store. Patience becomes a source of strength, a way of holding onto hope, and a reminder that every delay has a purpose.

In every season of life, proof that the journey matters is seen in the way we grow, in the strength we build, and in the ways we draw closer to God. The journey is not just a means to an end; it is a valuable part of God's plan for us, filled with lessons, blessings, and opportunities for growth.

Day 30 - Planting Seeds of Hope in Struggle

In life, we all go through struggles—times when it feels like we're walking uphill, carrying heavy burdens, or even stuck with no way out. In these moments, it can be hard to find hope, and we may wonder why we're facing so many challenges. But from a Biblical perspective, struggles are not only a part of life; they are also times when God plants seeds of hope within us that can grow into something beautiful and lasting. When we face hardships, God is with us, teaching us to lean on Him, to trust in His promises, and to believe that something good will come from even the darkest times. In Galatians 6:9, we find this encouragement: "And let us not be weary in well doing: for in due season we shall reap, if we faint not." This verse reminds us that our efforts are not wasted, that every act of faith and every step forward, even in struggle, is like planting a seed that will one day grow into a harvest of blessings. Planting seeds of hope in struggle matters because it helps us look beyond the pain of the moment and believe that God has a purpose for everything we go through. Each time we choose to have faith, to pray, or to keep moving forward, we are planting hope, a reminder that God's promises are true and that He will never leave us alone in our battles.

One of the reasons planting seeds of hope in struggle is so important is because it strengthens our faith. In James 1:2-3, we are reminded, "My brethren, count it all joy when ye fall into divers temptations; Knowing this, that the trying of your faith worketh patience." When we face trials, our faith is tested, and each time we choose to trust in God, that faith grows stronger. Struggles give us a chance to put our faith into action, to rely on God instead of our own understanding, and to believe that He is working in ways we cannot yet see. Each seed of hope we plant by choosing faith over fear, patience over frustration, and trust over doubt brings us closer to God, helping us to develop a faith that can withstand any storm. This growth of faith is a beautiful thing, showing us that with God, we are capable of far more than we ever imagined. Planting seeds of hope teaches us to believe that God is greater than our problems, that He is always with us, and that every struggle is an opportunity to deepen our relationship with Him.

Another reason planting seeds of hope matters is that it helps us to focus on God's promises rather than on our circumstances. In 2 Corinthians 5:7, Paul writes, "For we walk by faith, not by sight." This verse encourages us to look beyond what we can see, to trust in God's word, and to believe in His promises, even when the future looks uncertain. Struggles often make us feel limited by what we can see or control, but planting seeds of hope shifts our focus, helping us to remember that God's plans are bigger and better than our current situation. Each time we choose hope over despair, we are reminding ourselves of God's faithfulness, His goodness, and His power to bring beauty out of brokenness. These seeds of hope become anchors, helping us to stand firm in faith even when life feels uncertain, and teaching us to trust that God's promises are true, that His timing is perfect, and that He is always working on our behalf.

Planting seeds of hope in struggle also teaches us resilience, the strength to keep going even when things are tough. In Romans 5:3-4, we read, "And not only so, but we glory in tribulations also: knowing that tribulation worketh patience; And patience, experience; and experience, hope." Each struggle we face builds patience within us, and that patience leads to experience, which fills us with hope. This hope is not just a fleeting feeling; it's a strength that grows each time we overcome a challenge. Resilience is the ability to bounce back, to keep moving forward, and to believe that God's plans are worth the wait. Each seed of hope planted in struggle is a reminder that we are stronger than we think, that with God's help, we can overcome any obstacle, and that every moment of endurance brings us closer to the blessings God has for us. This resilience is like a tree growing strong roots, capable of withstanding any storm, and it's through planting seeds of hope that we become people of strength, people who can face the world with courage and faith.

In times of struggle, planting seeds of hope also helps us to find peace, knowing that God is in control. In Philippians 4:6-7, we are encouraged, "Be careful for nothing; but in every thing by prayer and supplication with thanksgiving let your requests be made known unto God. And the peace of God, which passeth all understanding, shall keep your hearts and minds through Christ Jesus." Each time we pray in times of struggle, we are planting seeds of hope, trusting that God hears us and that He will provide for us in His perfect way. This peace guards our hearts, reminding us that we are not alone and that God is taking care of us, even when life feels chaotic. Hope grows when we trust in God's peace, helping us to stay calm, to let go of worry, and to believe that God's love is greater than any fear or doubt. This peace is a gift that comes from knowing God is in control, that He holds our future, and that no struggle is too big for Him.

Another beautiful thing about planting seeds of hope in struggle is that it allows us to become a source of encouragement to others. When we go through hard times and find hope in God's promises, we become witnesses to His faithfulness, able to share that hope with those around us. In 2 Corinthians 1:3-4, we read, "Blessed be God, even the Father of our Lord Jesus Christ, the Father of mercies, and the God of all comfort; Who comforteth us in all our tribulation, that we may be able to comfort them which are in any trouble." Our struggles and the hope we find in them allow us to reach out to others, to offer words of encouragement, and to show them that God's love is real. Each seed of hope we plant becomes a light that shines for others, a reminder that they, too, can find peace and strength in God. By sharing our own experiences of hope, we help others to see that they are not alone, that there is always a reason to hold on, and that God is with them just as He is with us.

Finally, planting seeds of hope in struggle reminds us that God's plans are always greater than our present difficulties. In Jeremiah 29:11, God says, "For I know the thoughts that I think toward you, saith the Lord, thoughts of peace, and not of evil, to give you an expected end." This promise assures us that God has good plans for us, that He sees beyond our current pain, and that He is leading us toward a future filled with peace and blessing. Each seed of hope we plant in times of struggle is a declaration of faith, a way of saying, "God, I trust that Your plans are good." This hope gives us the strength to keep going, to believe that our struggles are temporary, and to know that God's blessings are on the way. Planting hope means looking forward, trusting that God is preparing something wonderful for us, and finding joy in the knowledge that He is always with us, guiding us toward His promises.

In every moment of struggle, planting seeds of hope helps us to grow stronger, to trust God more deeply, and to believe that His love is always with us. Each seed of hope is a step of faith, a reminder that God's promises are true, and that His plans for us are good. Through every challenge, we are becoming people of hope, people who can face any struggle with courage, faith, and the certainty that God is working all things together for our good.

Day 31 - Pathways to Renewal Through Perseverance

In life, there are times when we feel weary and worn down, like we've been pushing forward for so long that we have nothing left to give. Moments of frustration can feel overwhelming, especially when it seems like all our hard work and dedication aren't producing any results. But the Bible teaches us that even in these exhausting times, God has a purpose for our perseverance. Through the challenges, as we continue to push forward, God leads us down pathways of renewal, helping us grow stronger, building our character, and giving us the endurance to keep going. Perseverance is more than just pressing on; it is choosing to trust in God's promises, even when the road is tough and the outcome is unclear. In Isaiah 40:31, we find the beautiful promise, "But they that wait upon the Lord shall renew their strength; they shall mount up with wings as eagles; they shall run, and not be weary; and they shall walk, and not faint." This verse reminds us that when we choose to rely on God and keep going in faith, He renews our strength. Pathways to renewal through perseverance matter because they show us that God is with us, strengthening us every step of the way, and that He is faithful to refresh us, even in our hardest moments. Each time we persevere, we are choosing to believe that God has a purpose for our journey, that He is working within us, and that every step forward, no matter how small, is part of His plan to shape us into who He created us to be.

One reason perseverance is so powerful is that it builds resilience within us, giving us the strength to face future challenges with courage and hope. In Romans 5:3-4, we read, "And not only so, but we glory in tribulations also: knowing that tribulation worketh patience; And patience, experience; and experience, hope." Each struggle we endure becomes a stepping stone, helping us develop patience, which in turn builds experience and fills us with hope. Through perseverance, God teaches us to be strong, to keep pressing forward, and to find hope even when the way is hard. Every trial and frustration we face has a purpose, teaching us to trust God more fully and to see that with His strength, we can endure anything. This resilience becomes part of our character, helping us to become people who do not give up, who continue to trust in

God's promises, and who know that even in our darkest hours, God is still working. Resilience is a gift that grows each time we persevere, reminding us that we are not defined by our struggles but by our ability to overcome them through faith.

Perseverance also teaches us to lean on God's strength rather than our own. In 2 Corinthians 12:9, God tells Paul, "My grace is sufficient for thee: for my strength is made perfect in weakness." This verse reminds us that God's strength shines brightest when we feel weakest. Persevering through moments of frustration brings us closer to God, showing us that we don't have to carry every burden alone. Each time we choose to keep going, despite our exhaustion or discouragement, we are learning to rely on God's strength, to find comfort in His presence, and to trust that He will carry us through. Pathways to renewal through perseverance reveal to us that God's grace is more than enough and that His power is greatest when we are at our lowest. This reliance on God's strength changes us, helping us to live with confidence, knowing that He is with us and that He is our source of strength in every situation.

Another important aspect of perseverance is the way it builds our faith, teaching us to trust in God's timing and His plan. In Proverbs 3:5-6, we are encouraged, "Trust in the Lord with all thine heart; and lean not unto thine own understanding. In all thy ways acknowledge him, and he shall direct thy paths." Perseverance is an act of trust, a choice to keep moving forward even when we don't understand why things are happening the way they are. Each time we persevere, we are showing God that we trust Him, that we believe He is in control, and that we are willing to follow His lead. This deepens our faith, helping us to rely on God's wisdom rather than our own understanding and to believe that His timing is perfect, even when we can't see the whole picture. Persevering in faith shows us that God is guiding us, that He knows what is best, and that every delay or setback is part of His greater purpose for our lives.

Through perseverance, we also learn the power of hope. In Hebrews 10:36, we read, "For ye have need of patience, that, after ye have done the will of God, ye might receive the promise." This verse encourages us to hold onto hope, to believe that God's promises are true, and to trust that His blessings are coming. Each time we persevere, we are choosing hope, believing that God's plans for us are good and that He will fulfill His promises in His perfect time. This hope is a light that guides us, lifting our spirits and helping us to keep going, even when things seem impossible. Perseverance plants seeds of hope in our hearts, showing us that with God, there is always a reason to keep moving forward, always a future worth waiting for, and always a purpose in every struggle.

Perseverance also brings us closer to God, helping us to build a relationship with Him that is rooted in trust, love, and faith. In James 4:8, we are reminded, "Draw nigh to God, and he will draw nigh to you." As we persevere, we spend more time seeking God's presence, praying for His guidance, and relying on His promises. This closeness to God fills us with peace, reminding us that we are never alone and that He is always with us, guiding us through every challenge. Persevering in faith allows us to experience God's love in new ways, to feel His comfort in our hardest times, and to grow in our understanding of His grace. Each step we take in perseverance is a step closer to God, a chance to deepen our faith and to feel His presence in a real and personal way.

Finally, perseverance gives us the ability to encourage others, to show them that God's strength is real, and that His promises are worth holding onto. In 1 Thessalonians 5:11, we are encouraged, "Wherefore comfort yourselves together, and edify one another, even as also ye do." Our perseverance becomes a source of hope for those around us, a reminder that with God, all things are possible. When we share our stories of perseverance, we inspire others to keep going, to believe in God's promises, and to trust that He is with them. Our perseverance becomes a testimony of God's faithfulness, a light that shines for others, showing them that God is their strength and that His love is unchanging. Each time we persevere, we are not only growing in our faith but also helping others to see that God's grace is enough, that His power is real, and that His promises are true.

In every season of life, pathways to renewal through perseverance show us that God is with us, strengthening us, guiding us, and helping us to become the people He created us to be. Perseverance matters because it builds our character, deepens our faith, and fills us with hope. Through perseverance, we find renewal, discovering that God's love and grace are enough for every challenge we face. Each moment of perseverance is a reminder that with God, we can overcome anything, and that His plans for us are always worth the journey.

Conclusion

As we reach the end of "Why It Matters: Finding Hope in Moments of Frustration", let's pause and reflect on the journey we've taken together. This journey hasn't been easy; it's been one filled with honest confrontations, tears, and the raw feeling of wrestling with life's most painful questions. Frustration is not a mere inconvenience. It can feel like a weight on your spirit, a constant reminder of hopes unfulfilled, prayers unanswered, and dreams deferred. But now, as we stand here together, we know that frustration doesn't have to be the end of our story. In fact, it is often the beginning of something deeper, something that only God Himself can orchestrate—a transformation that reshapes not only our circumstances but our hearts and souls.

Every page of this book has been about one thing: finding meaning in the struggle, discovering purpose in the pain, and realizing that, even when life feels impossibly difficult, it all matters. You may have come here searching for answers, for a way to make sense of the things that keep you up at night, the frustrations that have threatened to steal your joy, and the setbacks that seem to keep you from moving forward. And maybe you still don't have all the answers. But perhaps you've found something even more valuable—a hope that goes beyond understanding, a renewed belief that God is working, even in ways we cannot see.

In this journey, we have seen that God is not silent in our struggles. He is present, even when we feel alone, and He hears every whispered prayer, every sigh of despair, every groan too deep for words. As it says in Romans 8:26, "The Spirit itself maketh intercession for us with groanings which cannot be uttered." Your struggles are heard, felt, and held by a God who cares, a God who collects each tear and uses each one to water the soil of your heart. Each tear is a seed that, in God's perfect time, will bring forth something beautiful and unexpected. God doesn't waste your pain; He transforms it, planting seeds of hope and resilience that will bloom in due season.

You may have found, through these pages, that hope is not about having all the answers or about seeing every prayer answered the way we desire. Hope is learning to trust in God's goodness, even when the path is unclear. Hope is choosing to believe that God is good, not because our circumstances are perfect but because He is. Hope is learning to wait, to trust, and to know that God's timing is always perfect. And this hope is not something flimsy or weak; it is a fierce, resilient trust that holds on even in the darkest times. It is the conviction that God is weaving every thread of our lives, even the messy and painful ones, into a tapestry more beautiful than we could ever imagine.

As you move forward from here, my prayer for you is that you will carry this hope with you as a light, a source of strength that fuels your journey. Let it remind you that even when life feels frustrating, when progress seems slow or nonexistent, and when setbacks seem to define your path, God is still writing your story. You are not forgotten, and your journey matters to Him. Every step, every stumble, every moment of doubt—all of it is shaping you into someone stronger, more compassionate, more connected to God.

Remember, too, that frustration doesn't have to define you. It may be part of your story, but it is not the whole story. Frustration is the soil in which faith can grow, the place where perseverance is born, and the training ground for resilience. As James 1:2-4 tells us, "My brethren, count it all joy when ye fall into divers temptations; Knowing this, that the trying of your faith worketh patience. But let patience have her perfect work, that ye may be perfect and entire, wanting nothing." Through every challenge, God is working something within you that is precious, something that will make you whole. You may not see it yet, but each frustration, each waiting season, is refining you, preparing you for the good things God has prepared for you.

The road ahead may still hold moments of hardship, days when you feel worn out, and seasons when hope feels faint. But now you have seen that there is power in persistence, in trusting God even when life doesn't make sense. You know that hope is not a fleeting feeling; it's a choice. You have learned that perseverance doesn't mean forcing yourself through life on your own but leaning into God's strength and letting Him carry you when you feel weak. And you have discovered that the journey itself is sacred, that God walks beside you, and that He is faithful to complete the work He began in you.

In closing, may you hold onto this truth: Your life matters. Your journey matters. Every step you take, every act of faith, every moment you hold on—it all matters to God. He is with you, closer than you could ever imagine, guiding you, comforting you, and cheering you on. So keep going. Even when it's hard, even when you feel tired, even when the way forward is unclear—keep going. Remember that God is a God of hope, a God who brings beauty out of brokenness, a God who redeems even the darkest nights. His love for you is unchanging, His promises are true, and His plans for you are good.

Let this be your anthem as you step forward: that God is with you, that He has purpose in every season, and that He is making all things new. Hold fast to hope, cling to His promises, and trust that your journey is unfolding exactly as it should. No matter how frustrated, lost, or weary you may feel, know that God sees you, loves you, and is guiding you toward a future filled with His grace, His joy, and His peace. In every frustration, find the courage to look up, to lift your eyes to the One who holds you and who will never let you go.

Don't miss out!

Visit the website below and you can sign up to receive emails whenever Joshua Rhoades publishes a new book. There's no charge and no obligation.

https://books2read.com/r/B-A-AJLBB-YSZIF

BOOKS 2 READ

Connecting independent readers to independent writers.

Did you love *Why It Matters- Finding Hope in Moments of Frustration"*? Then you should read *Enabled- Living God's Purpose With Power*[1] by Joshua Rhoades!

The 31-day devotional, "Enabled: Living God's Purpose With Power", is a refreshing and empowering guide for believers seeking to deepen their relationship with God and walk confidently in His purpose. Through a month-long journey, this devotional brings readers face-to-face with the profound truth that God equips, sustains, and strengthens us to fulfill His calling. Each daily message is centered on Scripture, rooted in the timeless wisdom of the King James Version, and inspired by I Timothy 1:12, where Paul says, "And I thank Christ Jesus our Lord, who hath enabled me." This verse forms the heart of this devotional, reminding us that just as God enabled Paul to overcome immense trials, He provides us with the strength to navigate our own challenges, live with courage, and stay faithful to His purpose.

---

1. https://books2read.com/u/3Lqy20

2. https://books2read.com/u/3Lqy20

Life often brings uncertainties, doubts, and fears that weigh us down, making us feel inadequate or overwhelmed. Yet, "Enabled" speaks directly to those struggles, encouraging readers to trade their weaknesses for God's boundless strength. Each day's entry includes a Scripture reflection, practical insight, and a heartfelt prayer, making it easy to apply God's truths to everyday life. This book is a powerful reminder that we are never meant to walk the Christian journey alone or rely solely on our own abilities. Rather, God's power is ever-present and available, actively working through us to accomplish His will. Through this devotional, you'll discover the peace that comes from knowing God's strength is made perfect in our weakness, allowing us to live with resilience, hope, and purpose.

As you progress through each day's message, you'll be encouraged by how God empowers us to overcome fear, endure difficult circumstances, serve others with love, and live courageously in every situation. By the end of the 31 days, you'll have a renewed understanding of how to rely on God's strength, not your own, and find that even in the toughest moments, His grace is always sufficient, His love never wavers, and His plans for you are steadfast. Each devotion highlights a unique aspect of God's enabling power, such as courage, peace, endurance, wisdom, and faithfulness, helping you see how His presence enriches every corner of life.

Whether you're facing challenges, feeling uncertain, or simply longing to strengthen your faith, "Enabled: Living God's Purpose With Power" is a perfect companion. This devotional guides you to keep your eyes on Christ, trust His timing, and walk with confidence, knowing you are equipped by His Spirit. It's a beautiful resource for anyone, whether new to the faith or well along in their walk with the Lord. With each day's entry, you'll find yourself empowered, encouraged, and equipped to live out God's calling in your life, discovering that His enabling power isn't just for the heroes of Scripture, but for every believer today—including you. This book becomes a personal guide and source of daily inspiration, helping you build a strong foundation in faith and a life transformed by God's presence.